GETTING THE BEST FROM

CHALKY GARDENS

GETTING THE BEST FROM

CHALKY GARDENS

PETER McHOY

SERIES EDITOR

ALAN TOOGOOD

WARD LOCK LIMITED · LONDON

First published in Great Britain in 1989 by Ward Lock Limited, 8 Clifford Street, London W1X 1RB, an Egmont Company.

Designed by David Robinson

Typeset by Jamesway Graphics Hanson Close Middleton Manchester M24 2HD

Printed and bound by Rotolito, Milan, Italy

British Library Cataloguing in Publication Data

McHoy, Peter, 1941–
    Getting the best from gardening on chalk.
    1. Gardens with chalk soils. Plants.
    Cultivation
    I. Title
    635. 9'55

ISBN 0 7063 6758 8

Previous page:
Spring at Highdown, near Goring in Sussex, showing how well a wide range of bulbs will grow on an alkaline soil. Daffodils and anemones do particularly well.

CONTENTS

INTRODUCTION

Like many other people, I used to think that alkaline (chalky) soils were a real problem – they are often portrayed that way. Gradually I realized that the problem lay less with the plants than with the attitude of the gardener. If you happen to hanker after rhododendrons or clamour for camellias, gardening on chalk or limestone can be frustrating, but whatever your soil there are some plants that won't like it. Come to terms with the fact that some plants will always struggle to survive in your garden, then the possibilities will proliferate.

This book will show you how to coax those reluctant growers, but the emphasis is on getting the best from your garden with the least effort – it's much easier to grow the less demanding plants that will actually *thrive,* than to try to spend time and money on what can be a disheartening struggle with that group of plants known as calcifuges (plants that dislike calcium, chalk or limestone, in the soil).

Gardening on an alkaline soil is most likely to be a problem if you have just moved home and are taking over a garden in a new area.

Gardeners who have always gardened on chalk need no convincing of the possibilities but someone who has never before had to contend with the special problems of these soils may initially find the prospect daunting.

This book will tell you how to deal with most of the practical problems that you are likely to encounter, and it suggests plenty of plants that will grow well on alkaline soils. For sheer inspiration, though, there is no substitute for visiting other people's gardens, to see what they have achieved. On pages 123–125 you will find a list of well-known gardens that share your kind of soil problems. Simply observing what works well for others in your neighbourhood can also be an inspiration.

Alkaline soils do create some problems, but they are no bar to an attractive garden.

There may be times when your soil appears to be a 'problem', but there are so many solutions available that it's not difficult to be positive in your approach. Some chalk gardens are the envy of others. This book sets out to show some of the possibilities, and hopefully to inspire you to garden with confidence and creativity.

This herbaceous border is on shallow soil in a garden created from an old chalk pit. Stately red-hot-pokers (kniphofias) are among the many plants that thrive.

SOIL CHART

How do I know I have an alkaline soil?

Ask the following questions.

Q:What's growing wild?

A:The soil is alkaline where the following plants are growing:

- Old man's beard *(Clematis vitalba)*
- Sweet violet *(Viola odorata)*
- Yew (Taxus baccata)

Q:What's growing over the fence?

A:If the following are growing in your neighbour's gardens, the soil is likely to be alkaline:

- Box *(Buxus sempervirens)*
- Carnations and other dianthus
- Lilac *(Syringa vulgaris)*
- Spindle tree *(Euonymus europaeus)*
- Clematis

Q:What's the countryside like?

A:If you live in or near one of the following types of countryside, there is a possibility that the soil in your garden is alkaline. However, bear in mind that this does not always apply, so use other indicators too.

Old Man's Beard

Sweet Violet

Yew tree

• Hilly areas, especially in the North Downs of Kent and Surrey, and the South Downs of Sussex, the Chilterns, Wiltshire, and some parts of Yorkshire.

• Hilly or coastal areas where white rock is exposed (white cliffs in Kent, chalk figures carved into the hillside in Wiltshire, etc).

• A whitish appearance to ploughed fields (where pieces of chalk have been brought to the surface by the plough).

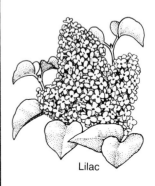

Lilac

Q:What can the soil tell me?

A:There is a good chance the soil is alkaline if:

• Pieces of white chalk lie near the surface or are exposed by raking.

• You come to a layer of whitish rock when you dig.

• The soil is shallow and dries out quickly.

Spindle tree

Q:How can I be sure?

A:Use one of the inexpensive soil testing kits that you can buy from garden centres. This will give you a sure indication within minutes.

Carnation

THE PROBLEMS AND THE POSSIBILITIES

*T*HE Attempt to grow unsuitable plants on a very alkaline soil and you will almost certainly be disappointed. Anyone who has tried it will instantly recognize the symptoms: poor, often stunted growth, and yellowish leaves that lack the good colouring of a healthy plant.

There are other handicaps. Chalky soils are often shallow, which means that trees and large shrubs may be vulnerable in high winds. Cultivation may also prove difficult because of the underlying rock and perhaps many pieces of chalk in the topsoil and the soils are often found in hilly districts, and shallow soils on slopes dry out quickly.

Digging a hole for planting a tree or a shrub can bring home starkly what a handicap these soils can be. The topsoil is often stony and difficult to dig, and as little as 30 cm (1 ft) or less down, a pickaxe may be needed to break up the stone beneath. That, and the chemical effects alkalinity has on the availability of nutrients, is what you have to overcome.

Kiftsgate Court—a neighbour of Hidcote, that other famous alkaline garden in Gloucestershire.

ON THE BRIGHT SIDE

One can't ignore the problems, but the negative side has been presented first only to get it out of the way to be able to concentrate on the more positive aspects. Some of my favourite gardens are on chalky soils – one, the famous garden of the late Sir Frederick Stern, at Highdown near Worthing in Sussex, was created out of an old chalk pit. It's true that some of the plants do show signs of chlorosis, but most of them thrive and even some of the plants that do show deficiency symptoms, such as the peonies, still provide a magnificent display.

I have, within half an hour's drive, some truly magnificent chalk gardens on the one hand and acid gardens where rhododendrons thrive on the other. Most of the plants are different on the two soil types, but it would be difficult to say that one garden is superior to the others. They are simply different.

The key to successful gardening is in part the overall sense of design and in part the ability to choose plants that do well and look good together. In the chapters that follow, these two aspects are related to the particular problems of alkaline soils, but

inspiration often comes best from looking at other people's gardens . . . from those who have, perhaps by a fair degree of trial and error, learned what can be best achieved.

The appendix on page 123 lists some famous gardens created in chalk or limestone areas, and it's worth making a point of visiting these, not only to note what grows well but perhaps to discover new plants too. Seeing plants growing is always better than reading descriptions in books, magazines, or catalogues. It's difficult to know whether you'll like a plant from a written description – when you see it you know instantly.

Famous gardens are often on the grand scale, but you will know which types of plants are likely to do well, and it's often possible to copy plant combinations from a small part of a large border.

Don't be afraid to experiment. Sometimes the results are surprising, and except in areas where the pH (see page 19) is exceptionally high you may find that theoretically 'difficult' plants will grow. Be wary of sweeping generalizations too. It's true that most magnolias dislike alkaline soils, yet you can find *M. highdownensis* and *M.* x *loebneri* doing very well on shallow chalk soils; most heathers prefer an acid soil, yet the invaluable winter-flowering *Erica carnea* is surprisingly lime-tolerant (though not recommended for shallow chalk soils).

'Borderline' plants may do well with just a bit of encouragement – perhaps lots of peat and compost incorporated at planting time and regular mulching afterwards.

There are tips for growing lime-haters in Chapter 8, but working against nature rather than with it means the rewards are sometimes small, and the effort and cost often appears great.

If you feel compelled to grow acid-loving plants such as rhododendrons and camellias, try them in tubs or raised beds, where it's possible to give them the kind of compost that they like.

A PLAN OF CAMPAIGN

Pick up any book on problem soils, and you will soon begin to wonder how it's possible to obtain enough garden compost or bulky organic manures. No matter how voluminous your kitchen waste, how good you are at mastering the intricacies of the compost heap, or how many friends you happen to have with horses, the chances are there won't be enough.

And if you live in a large town, stable manure and farmyard manure are scarce commodities. If you buy bagged manures, or opt for peat or perhaps pulverized bark, the cost can become prohibitive for a large area.

Skimp on your effort to improve the soil, and the effect on plant growth may be negligible.

It's sensible to concentrate your effort in just a few areas. Perhaps in the vegetable plot, or a small bed where you want to grow some of the more temperamental plants. Certainly effort – and compost – must go into getting new plants off to a good start.

Don't become too obsessed with compost and manure. They are always worth using, but if you want to keep cost in mind there may be other options to achieve worthwhile results more cheaply. Concentrating on plants that are naturally adapted to alkaline soils will mean that they need less coaxing – some will be happy on dry, shallow, and probably impoverished soil. If you garden on a hillside with a shallow soil that dries out quickly (typical of chalk downland), a simple irrigation system may achieve a dramatic improvement in the range of plants that will thrive in your garden.

MAKING THE MOST OF YOUR SOIL

Don't dismiss this chapter as irrelevant if your interest happens to lie in the plants themselves rather than the science that lies behind the good cultivation. It holds the key to getting the best from your garden. To appreciate *why* some plants do well while others cling only tenuously to life is to know how to minimize the mistakes and make the most of the plants in your garden.

Far left: *The famous garden of Hidcote Manor, with a white philadelphus contrasting well with the lavender.*
Left: *A mixed border at Mottisfont Abbey in Hampshire.*

Identifying a problem can help you solve it. Sometimes the obvious is obscured and the solution not as simple as the evidence would suggest. Alkaline soils cause an iron deficiency in many plants, but simply adding iron to the soil may not be the solution; some plants don't do well on chalk, yet the effect may be an indirect one – it could be micro-organisms that live in association with the host plant that dislike a high pH rather than the plant itself. Soil is a complex structure with many chemical and biological checks and balances. The soil is a life-support system far more than a simple anchorage for roots.

This chapter contains plenty of hints on how to identify alkaline soils, and what you can do to improve them. But it's always worth bearing in mind that steps taken to overcome an immediate problem (e.g. adding specific fertilisers if these are deficient) should be accompanied by measures to improve the overall physical structure and qualities of the soil. Improving the soil's depth and structure will often do much to alleviate the problems.

WHAT IS AN ALKALINE SOIL?

For convenience all alkaline soils are often referred to as 'chalk soils' (for conciseness we have sometimes done so in this book), but many alkaline soils are not derived from chalk, and the problems and the possibilities are slightly different. So measuring the pH of the soil, to tell you how acid or alkaline it is, will not actually tell you what *type* of soil you have.

An alkaline soil simply contains too much lime for some plants. But the lime (calcium carbonate) is derived from different sources.

Chalk is the purest form of calcium carbonate, derived from the skeletons and shells of myriads of marine creatures. The deposits may be several hundred feet deep (the white cliffs of Dover are an example), and the soil over them is frequently very shallow, sometimes as little as 10 cm (4in) on the slope of a hill, but much deeper at the bottom of a valley, where it has accumulated over the centuries. There are some famous figures carved out of chalk hills, which is possible because the chalk has such a shallow covering of soil and grassy turf.

Soils that overlie chalk rocks are likely to be very alkaline, often with a pH of 8 or more.

Limestone is a very hard form of calcium carbonate, and less absorbent than chalk. The soil that overlies it may be less alkaline (perhaps pH7.5), but more importantly there is often a greater depth of soil. In places, however, the rock comes to the surface as outcrops, a feature of the landscape in limestone areas.

Limy clay is found in a few areas (parts of Cheshire and Worcestershire in England for instance). This is sometimes known as 'marl', but it's best to avoid this confusing term as it is also used to describe a topdressing used on sports fields. Limy soils that occur in areas where the underlying rock is not limestone or chalk may even have been transported by wind, water, or glaciers, over millions of years. Limy clays may have the added problem of poor drainage.

Other alkaline soils include silts, and in some coastal areas sandy soils with a high proportion of disintegrated sea shells. These soils clearly have different structural properties from, say, chalk downland, and while our choice of recommended plants is still valid, some of the suggested measures to improve the *structure* of the soil may not be relevant.

Although rare, it is possible to have the problem of a very high pH even in areas where the soil is not naturally alkaline. I once took on an allotment and was staggered to find that even the cabbages were so chlorotic that I had to foliar feed with iron to restore their healthy green colour! As my neighbours had no problem, there had to be an explanation. It came in the form of a revelation that the previous owner used to do very well at the local show, which at that time gave bags of lime as prizes. Clearly reluctant to see waste or to give them away, he used them all . . . until gradually his crops began to fail and he ceased to win prizes and gave up the allotment in disgust. So if you have taken on a new garden and many of the plants look chlorotic, check the pH level of the soil.

Measuring the problem. You will know from the area in which you live, which *type* of soil you have, but measure the pH in order to determine the severity of the problem (see page 19).

MEASURING pH

The alkalinity or acidity of your soil can easily be measured with simple kits or meters. The reading is given on a scale (known as the pH scale) that ranges from 1 to 14, values less than 7 being acid, values higher than 7 alkaline. Soil in temperate areas is rarely lower than pH4 or higher than pH8. At first glance, numerically this may not seem a large difference, but the scale is logarithmic and a soil with a pH of 8 is 10 times more alkaline than one with a pH of 7, and 100 times more alkaline than one with a pH of 6. This puts into perspective the need for a fair degree of accuracy when reading colour charts with pH kits, and getting an accurate reading from a pH meter.

pH meters are the quickest and easiest to use. Although individual models may vary slightly, you generally have to clean the probe then push it into moist soil – after a short time the pH can be read off on the dial. The accuracy of these meters depends on the quality of the product, and some experts prefer to use colour comparators for accuracy. However, if you're colour blind, or want a quick and easy rough guide, a meter is probably a good choice.

Northbourne Court, a chalk garden in Kent, showing how lushly suitable plants will grow on an alkaline soil.

A

Fig 1a. Meters are quick to use but need care to achieve an accurate reading

Colour comparator kits are easy to use, but a bit more bother – and with some soils you may find it difficult to decide which colour on the chart the solution best matches.

Generally, samples are taken from the top 5-8 cm (2-3 in) of soil with a clean spoon, and the soil spread out to dry a little if very wet, any stones or fibrous material being removed. The right amount of soil is then put into a test-tube, an indicator solution is added, and the tube is shaken vigorously.

Lots of fine particles in suspension cloud the solution, and some kits use a filter system, or a chemical such as barium sulphate to help them settle out of the solution.

With all these kits you will have a colour chart against which to compare the solution – carefully follow any advice given with the kit about viewing position and light, otherwise it's easy to misread the shade.

Never depend on the reading from just one part of the garden. Not only can soil vary, but fertilizers and manures that you have applied to localized areas may give a reading that's not typical of the rest of the garden. It may also be worth taking a sample from a little deeper down if you think that mulches and perhaps leaching by rain may have significantly reduced the pH of the top inch or so.

If you garden on chalk, you won't need a kit or meter to tell you – it will be obvious. But testing your soil pH is useful for confirming other types of alkaline soil, and even in chalk gardens it can be helpful to know just how alkaline the soil is in particular parts of the garden. Sometimes there are areas that are much less alkaline, and these may be the places to grow some of those less tolerant plants.

HOW TO IMPROVE THINGS

Attempts to reduce the pH of the soil significantly on a large scale will almost certainly fail. As there are so many good plants that will thrive anyway, it just isn't worth the cost and effort to try. There are tips for growing lime-hating plants on page 28, but unless you want to make your gardening a struggle it's more sensible to put effort into improving the *structure* of the soil rather than trying to alter the pH.

Bulky organic material is almost universally beneficial – whether you garden on an alkaline clay or a quick-draining shallow chalk soil. On the one hand it can help to

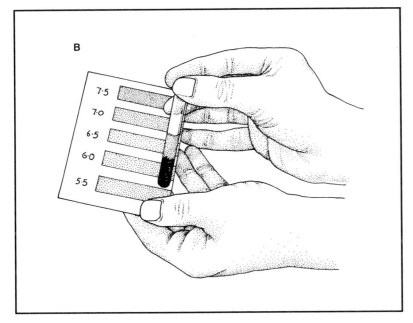

Fig 1b. It's always worth checking the pH of your soil – even if you know it's alkaline, it's helpful to know *how* alkaline it is in various parts of the garden. Simple kits in which you compare the shade of an extract of the soil sample against a colour card, are perfectly adequate for most purposes.

improve the structure and drainage of heavy clay, and on the other improve the structure and water-absorbing and nutrient-holding capacity of a light soil. In either case you will grow better plants as a result.

You will almost certainly never have as much as you would like, so use it mainly for new planting, and as a thick mulch for those plants unable to tolerate dry conditions (see pages 119 to 121), or for long established plants that seem unhappy.

Compost everything that you can, including much of the kitchen waste. Unless you produce considerably more garden compost than the average gardener (some enthusiasts grow crops such as comfrey just to compost, but you need a big garden to be able to do this), you'll have to buy in your supplies of manure or compost.

As you need a lot to make a real impression, it's worth checking costs locally before deciding what to use. If you have a brewery down the road then spent hops may be the best option; local stables or farms may provide a cheap source of manure, and so on.

A lorry load of spent mushroom compost from a local mushroom grower can be an economic way of obtaining a large quantity of bulky organic material. But as chalk or limestone is an ingredient of mushroom compost some experts don't recommend its use on alkaline soils. This is sensible advice if you are trying to reduce the alkalinity, but if you are simply trying to improve the *structure* and *water-holding* capacity of the soil for lime-tolerant plants, don't be afraid to use it. It won't actually make a highly alkaline soil any more alkaline.

Being naturally acid, peat is ideal for areas where you are trying to reduce alkalinity. It becomes expensive to use if you have a large garden, though buying in bulk from a peat supplier may reduce the cost (try looking among the small advertisements in gardening magazines). Moss peats are usually more acid than sedge peats.

If you use growing bags for tomatoes, or perhaps ornamentals on the patio, these will provide a useful source of peat for the garden later. Don't expect the peat to be very acid, because the pH will have been raised to somewhere near neutral for the growing bag, but it will probably have cost you no more than pure peat and you'll have had a season or two of use as a growing medium into the bargain.

A predominantly yellow border at Kiftsgate, with several euphorbias and the bold foliage effect of a rodgersia.

On the vegetable plot, green manuring (sowing a leafy crop such as mustard or even ryegrass, and digging it in before it seeds) will help. The plants provide humus for the soil as they decay.

IMPROVING FERTILITY

Improving fertility will help all plants, whether or not they are lime-tolerant. Chalk and limestone soils are generally poor and 'hungry', partly because a high pH suits many of the microbes that break down organic matter. Even if you apply lots of garden compost or manure, it is soon broken down and used up (this is not an excuse for not bothering to use any – it just means that you have to apply lots of it . . . frequently).

The pH of a soil affects the availability of certain nutrients. Among the major elements, phosphorus tends to tail off on very alkaline soils, while the availability of some minor or trace elements, such as iron and magnesium, falls off very rapidly. On mineral soils (not peaty soils), most nutrients are at their most available at a pH of 6.5, which is why this is regarded as horticulturally neutral rather than the strictly neutral 7.

It does not necessarily

mean that there is not enough of a particular nutrient in the soil, but that much of it is chemically locked in a form that makes it unavailable to the plants. That's why adding more sulphate of iron (ferrous sulphate) is not a solution to iron deficiency on chalky soils. It has to be applied in a form that will not become chemically locked and unavailable – these chelates (sold under the trade name Sequestrene) remain stable in the soil for many months. The iron is protected by molecules that hold it in a form available to plants.

Nitrogen is often deficient on chalky soils simply because it is quickly leached away after heavy rain. It's always worth applying a general balanced fertilizer until plants are established and growing well. It's better to apply a little several times during the growing season than to make one heavy application in spring.

Most bought compound or balanced fertilizers should be satisfactory, but it's best to avoid those few straight fertilizers that actually increase alkalinity. Nitro-chalk in particular should be avoided because it contains lime; if you want a straight nitrogenous fertilizer use sulphate of ammonia instead as this increases acidity.

Superphosphate is sometimes referred to as superphosphate of lime, but it contains calcium sulphate not calcium carbonate, and it won't make your ground more alkaline.

Foliar feeding overcomes many of the problems associated with lime-induced deficiencies (see page 117), but they are best regarded as a pick-me-up for plants that are not doing well, rather than as a normal routine.

SHALLOW SOILS

Shallow chalk soils will benefit from any increase in depth. If the chalk rock is only just beneath the surface, the roots will soon be in direct contact with the chalk. Apart from making conditions even more inhospitable for lime-haters, the shallowness of the soil means that most plants are likely to suffer in dry weather, and the shallow rooting may make trees and large shrubs particularly vulnerable in very strong winds.

New beds and borders will benefit from deep digging – though this is a relative term as it may be difficult to penetrate more than one spit (depth of a spade's blade) deep. The important point is to break up the hard layer of

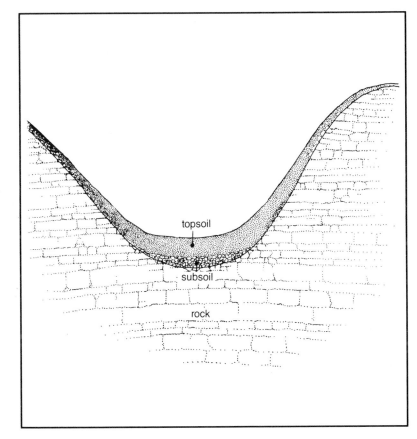

Fig 2. Many alkaline soils are in hilly areas. If you garden at the bottom of a valley, the soil will be deeper and gardening easier; high on the hillsides there may only be a very thin covering of soil over the alkaline rocks.

Below: Fig 3. Double digging will help to increase the depth of fertile, workable soil. Break up the subsoil (second spit) with a fork – or pickaxe if necessary – before turning over the next row as indicated by the arrows. To start double digging, take out the first trench of topsoil and barrow it to the far end of the plot to fill in the last trench.

chalk as much as possible. You may have to resort to a pick-axe – perhaps in the planting hole for a tree. Loosen it, but always ensure that you *do not bring more chalk to the surface*.

It will help if you can fork in plenty of compost or rotted manure, but don't put a thick layer of it at the bottom, compressed by soil on top. It will be more beneficial worked through the whole depth of the topsoil.

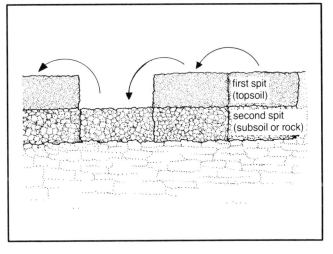

PLANTING HOLES

Even on shallow soils it should be possible to plant annuals and border perennials with a trowel and little trouble. But trees and shrubs need more.

On soils where the rock is close to the surface, remove a generous area of soil (make the hole wider than you would normally, to compensate for the fact that the roots will have to explore horizontally more than they would normally), and put this on one side. If possible break up the hard rock at the bottom with a pick-axe (perfectly feasible with soft chalk, but it may not be very practical with a hard limestone). You don't need to break it up into fine pieces, just open it up enough to give the roots a chance to explore more deeply.

Mix some peat or soil into the broken-up rock, and add plenty of peat or compost to the excavated soil that is to be returned to the planting hole.

If you are planning to insert a supporting stake, make sure you have broken enough rock to be able to insert it, *before you return the soil.*

After planting, and tying to a supporting stake if necessary, water thoroughly and then mulch thickly (don't do it the other way round, as the mulch may become soaked but the ground beneath remain comparatively dry). If you don't want to use a mulch such as compost or pulverized bark, use a planting square made of plastic or a butyl type material. These are simply squares of material that prevent weed growth. There are some types that let water seep through while still reducing evaporation and preventing weed growth. This kind of material comes in a strip that you could use for a whole shrub border.

Mulches of this type needn't look unattractive. Just cover them with some pulverized bark or gravel.

DEALING WITH STONES

Chalk and limestone soils may have lots of stones near the surface. They can make cultivating frustrating (even hoeing can become tiresome if you keep striking stones), but there's no point in attempting to remove them from borders – more will just work their way to the surface with further cultivation.

They are much more of a hazard in lawns, where they may cause injury to children playing on the grass as well as damage to mowing equipment. This is one place where it's sensible to remove as many as you can.

Many of them can be

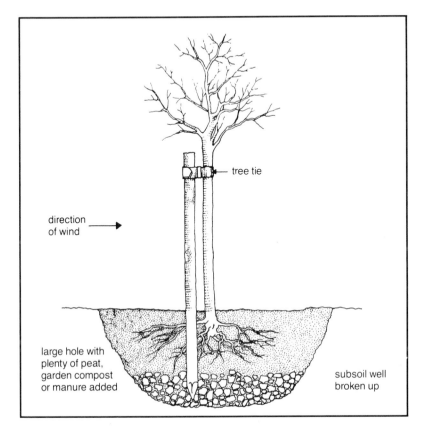

direction
of wind ➡

tree tie

large hole with
plenty of peat,
garden compost
or manure added

subsoil well
broken up

Fig 4a. Chalky soils are often shallow, and trees need special care when planting. Take out a large hole, and break up the subsoil to increase the depth that roots can penetrate easily. Add plenty of peat, garden compost, or manure, especially into the topsoil. Support with a stake and tree-ties, placing the stake on the side of the prevailing wind.

removed when preparing the ground for a lawn by raking the levelled surface first one way and then the other. Although more will work their way to the surface later, because the ground is not being turned and cultivated once the lawn is established, the problem will not be so acute. Nevertheless, even an established lawn will benefit from a 'picking over'. This seemingly formidable hands-and-knees task is accomplished with relative ease if you can get the whole family to work across the lawn with you, from one end to the other. I've even helped clear a football pitch of stones this way, and with enough willing helpers it's not an onerous task . . . and it will need repeating only infrequently.

IF YOU CAN'T RESIST

No matter how logical it is to grow only those plants that tolerate lime, especially when there is such a wide range of good ones to grow, most of us are still inclined to persevere with a few plants that clearly don't like what we have to offer them.

If you really do want to grow lime-haters, it's better to make special provision for them, even if it's demanding in effort and expense, rather than have sickly-looking plants dotted all around the garden.

For an isolated established plant that you don't want to move, foliar feeding and treating with chelated trace elements (see page 117) will probably keep them reasonably healthy-looking. If you're starting with a new plant, it's more satisfactory to provide a neutral or acid soil in just that part of the garden.

Digging in plenty of peat at planting time helps only in the short-term. Even if alkaline water does not seep in from all around the prepared planting area, the roots are almost certain to go down into the more alkaline soil or rock below.

A few determined enthusiasts line a large excavation with plastic or butyl before filling the hole with a non-alkaline compost in an attempt to reduce contamination from the surrounding soil. As holes or slits are essential to ensure free drainage and avoid waterlogging, there is still the risk of alkaline drainage water seeping in, especially if the garden is on a slope, and it's a troublesome way to grow a plant.

Fig 4b. You can try growing a lime-hating shrub in a specially prepared planting pit. Use thick polythene or butyl to line the hole, and fill it with lime-free soil or compost. Make sure there are drainage holes, otherwise the area might become waterlogged.

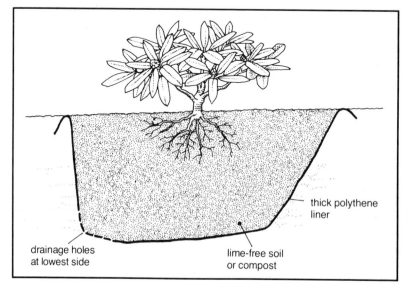

thick polythene liner

drainage holes at lowest side

lime-free soil or compost

If you do want to try this, you will need to excavate a hole large enough for the root-ball when the tree or shrub is several years old, before lining it with thick polythene. Avoid a saucer-shape (the sides will be too shallow at the edges); make it with straight sides and with a slope in one direction at the base – on the downhill side. Make plenty of drainage holes or slits along this bottom edge. If you want to be extra cautious, dust the hole with flowers of sulphur (which will neutralize any surrounding alkalinity) before inserting the liner.

You will have the cost of filling the liner with a neutral or acid compost, and you should ask yourself whether it would just be better to grow your plants in large containers.

Shrubs can be very effective in suitable containers; even small trees, like some of the maples, can be grown very successfully.

Good quality, frost-proof, large terracotta containers can be expensive. Often cheaper, and just as good, are half barrels. You can sometimes buy these from garden centres and shops, and even garages sometimes. Just keep your eyes open for them. They are good because they are fairly wide and stable, and hold a reasonable amount of compost. Some of the larger concrete containers are dependable and practical, but can look very municipal.

Don't expect shrubs in containers to grow as large as those in good soil in the open ground, but provided they are watered regularly they will at least look healthy. And a little restraint is sometimes no bad thing. Rhododendron 'Pink Pearl' can grow into a huge shrub far too large for a modern town garden, yet I have one in a tub that will take years before it outgrows its welcome, and it flowers profusely every year.

Raised beds are another option, but I think they should always look part of the design. I have seen peaty raised beds in chalk gardens that spoil the garden – they look wrong if they are simply added in odd corners to provide a home for some acid-loving plants.

Raised beds that you would have as part of the design *anyway,* even if you filled them with lime-loving plants, are a different matter. They will look *right,* and you have the ideal opportunity to provide an acid soil or compost for those more sensitive plants if you decide you want to grow them.

DESIGNING A CHALK GARDEN

There are many different kinds of alkaline soil, and if you happen to garden on an alkaline clay on a flat plain, or on an alkaline sand by the coast, much of the advice in this chapter may seem irrelevant. It is intended primarily for those having to cope with chalk or limestone geology, which usually means slopes and shallow soil, which create their own garden design problems.

A book like this cannot attempt to deal with garden design in detail, but whether starting from scratch or modifying an existing garden, it's worth looking at the design as an

Far right: *Part of the rock garden at Preston Park, Brighton, created an a chalky hillside using limestone rocks. The blue rock campanulas thrive in these conditions.*
Right: *A berberis in fruit. Most berberis will do well on a wide range of soils, and they are among the most useful all-round shrubs.*

overall concept rather than simply a solution to a cultivation problem. Raised beds that are not integrated, terraces that are out of proportion, and beds and borders created without regard to some larger plan, will not make a well-designed garden. There are many books on garden design that explain the principles of design: including the use of grids and focal points. All these sound principles can be applied to chalk and limestone gardens, but the majority of gardeners are probably happy to settle for a modification to their existing garden in preference to a major reconstruction of all the garden.

Whatever the size or shape of your garden, it's worth deciding on the *style* that you prefer – formal or informal; colourful but high-maintenance or less colourful and low maintenance; lots of hard landscaping or mainly beds and borders with the emphasis on plants.

FORMAL OR INFORMAL?

Formal gardens generally need much more maintenance. Lawns need to be trim if they are not to look neglected; regular pruning and trimming of shrubs and border plants will probably be necessary if formal outlines are to be maintained; and much more weeding and regular replanting is likely to be necessary. Certainly, spring and summer bedding will call for additional work at least twice a year. It's an effort you might not begrudge for the colour and strong sense of design that a formal garden can bring. Certainly, most annual bedding plants and even hardy annuals, being shallow-rooting, will do well on chalk. And the major bulbs, such as daffodils and tulips, but many more too, can thrive in chalk gardens.

Informality can be irritating to anyone with an attitude of mind that likes neatness and organization. But shrub borders underplanted with drifts of anemones and mixed groundcover, and borders that somehow mix shrubs, border perennials, and annuals in a happy medley, like many cottage gardens, have a charm of their own.

There's much to be said for the informal style of gardening if you have a difficult site. Plants that can adapt and do well can take over as the less tolerant ones fail to thrive, and die out. I have several beds in a gravel garden that evolve each year. I was quite pleased with my initial planting, but by leaving the plants to sort themselves out, the least suited have died out and those that like the conditions best have thrived and spread to take over the gaps left by the failures. The results are beds with changing populations, but they are colourful all summer and I have not had to intervene (or even weed) for years. Plants can't be given such freedom from intervention in a formal garden design.

With an informal approach, bulbs can be left to naturalize – not only in grass, but also to form a carpet of colour among the shrubs in spring.

Groundcover of all kinds is especially valuable for chalk and limestone gardens. Many groundcover plants will provide cover in places where larger border plants would fail to thrive, or where cultivation might be difficult. Use them to cover an area with very thin soil, or on steep slopes that would be difficult to cultivate.

Don't dismiss groundcover plants as dull. A steep, sunny bank with stony or dry soil can become a veritable dazzling blaze of colour with sun roses (helianthemums) in

early summer, in shades of red, yellow, orange and pink. The rose of Sharon (*Hypericum calycinum*) can transform a dry chalk bank into a carpet of yellow (and you have good evergreen cover for the whole year). If this is not imaginative enough, try letting some pink rambling or carpeting roses scramble over the bank with the hypericum.

Difficult sites needn't mean dull gardens.

MAKING THE MOST OF A SLOPE

Because many chalk and limestone gardens are in hilly

Fig 5. It may be possible to increase the depth of good soil, and make a feature at the same time, by forming slightly raised beds on a slope. Circular ones have been used here, to give the garden a stronger sense of design.

Fig 6. A slope provides an opportunity to use various design techniques, such as steps, raised beds (which you can fill with a neutral soil), and paved terraces on which you can grow plants in containers (in which you can use a compost that suits the plants that you want to grow).

areas, slopes are a common feature. It may be possible to make the most of the slope by creating a water feature with cascades that really do look natural. Combined with a rock garden, they can look extremely convincing.

Rock gardens are another natural for a sloping garden, though a shady north-facing slope is not really suitable. In some limestone districts, the rock outcrops come to the surface naturally, and as you can do little to remove these it's best to build a rock feature around them. There are many wonderful alpine plants that thrive very well in limestone rock gardens.

Rock gardens and cascades can look pretentious in small gardens, and it may be best to take a more formal approach, perhaps with terraces.

Terracing always adds interest to a garden, especially if you have to wind your way round sloping paths or up short flights of steps to explore the next level. But it's hard work to create, and probably expensive in materials if you have to build retaining walls and perhaps want to pave some of the levels.

Bear in mind that if you have terraces with lawns at the higher levels, you will need access via a slope for the mower, unless, of course, you use a lightweight hover mower that you can carry up the steps easily.

As a general rule it's worth trying to take the eye across a sloping garden as well as up it. A focal point at one corner is likely to be more successful than one that takes the eye straight up (or down) the slope to the end of the garden in a direct line. Terraces are usually improved if they are linked by staggered steps,

Above: Fig. 7 Raised beds and containers provide plenty of opportunities for growing plants that don't like an alkaline soil. You can provide neutral or even acid conditions, in small areas for those more demanding plants.

Left: Fig 8. If raised beds are used, it's worth making an effort to integrate them into the overall design. Here railway sleepers (ties) have been used for the raised beds, to link them with the paved area.

sometimes on the left, sometimes on the right, rather than going straight up the centre: it adds interest when you have to meander to explore the garden.

HARD LANDSCAPING

Small gardens, whether or not they are on a slope, lend themselves to more hard landscaping. Patios and other paved areas throw the emphasis onto raised beds and containers anyway, and this gives you much more control over the soil. If you are prepared to buy in compost or topsoil for raised beds and containers, you have the choice of growing lime-haters or lime-lovers as the whim takes you.

To create a partly paved garden you will have to excavate some of the soil, and some of the topsoil can be used to increase the depth of beds and borders where the soil is shallow. But it's essential to use only the top few inches of soil for this. Avoid spreading the lower and

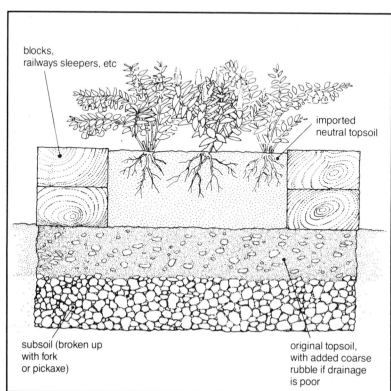

blocks, railways sleepers, etc

imported neutral topsoil

subsoil (broken up with fork or pickaxe)

original topsoil, with added coarse rubble if drainage is poor

Fig 9. Don't just add a raised bed without preparing the ground beneath first – deep rooted plants will soon start to penetrate soil at the original ground level.

Fig 10. If you create a raised bed like this, it should be possible to grow acid-loving shrubs such s rhododendrons, camellias, and heathers.

almost certainly more alkaline subsoil around areas of the garden.

If you like a challenge and really do want to grow some of the larger acid-loving shrubs, such as rhododendrons and camellias, raised beds can be successful—provided you locate them at a high spot where alkaline drainage water will not gradually raise the pH. But these large shrubs look silly in small raised beds (it's better to choose compact varieties and grow them in tubs). For an acid bed to be worthwhile it needs to be fairly large (though not necessarily more than 30-45 cm (1-1½ ft) high. Railway sleepers (ties) can look good and the proportions are right if you are making a fairly substantial raised bed. But if you use railway sleepers (ties) for a raised bed, the garden will look more designed if you can incorporate them into other parts of the design (perhaps in combination with pavers or bricks for the patio surface). The same principle applies generally: try to incorporate the materials used for any raised beds into the paving or other features. If you use concrete paving slabs for the patio, bricks for the path, and railway sleepers (ties) for the raised beds, the garden won't look either integrated or well designed.

BACKBONE PLANTS

Having spent many years visiting some excellent chalk gardens regularly, I have never been in doubt that even the most 'difficult' alkaline soils present no real problem when it comes to the sheer range of good plants that can be grown. My own observations were reinforced when I was once involved in a survey of gardeners with so-called 'problem' chalk or limestone soils. They were asked which plants they found did well in their garden, and the list that was produced covered the vast majority of plants that you'll find in any garden with a good neutral loam. To produce a short and concise list, it would have been easier to ask what did *not* do well.

What is more significant is that a shrub that one person might describe as unsuccessful another would recommend. This is not as contradictory as it might seem. *Soil pH is only part of the picture:* soil depth and structure can influence the performance of many plants. Some shrubs may do well on shallow chalk soils but not necessarily on acid clays;

Right: Buddleia davidii, *aptly known as the butterfly bush. A really easy shrub that often thrives in the most unpromising positions. This variety is 'Nanhoe Purple'.*
Opposite: Cistus ladaniferus, *a super shrub for a sunny and sheltered position. But not one for a cold district.*

with the less hardy plants climate may be as important as soil; others may grow reasonably well for a few years on alkaline soils, but then tend to die prematurely.

A vast number of shrubs will grow satisfactorily over a wide pH range, from acid to alkaline. Berberis and pyracanthas for example. Factors such as prolonged low winter temperatures, or drought in summer, may have a bigger impact on some shrubs than the pH of the soil.

The same versatility applies to many trees, which even if they cannot send down roots very deeply on some chalk soils manage to achieve sufficient anchorage by spreading them widely. Only in exceptional gales are they likely to be at risk – even then isolated trees, and those at the edge of a group of established trees, are surprisingly stable because of the wide root spread. The most vulnerable are the inner trees that are exposed once the outer shield trees have fallen: as the once-in-a-lifetime gale that hit southern England in October 1987 showed, those that have not had the room to form a good spreading root system will fall like skittles on shallow soils.

This chapter is about the backbone plants of any garden: the trees and shrubs that form the framework against which other plants are viewed. No matter how many bulbs will do well, or how brilliant the summer bedding, unless a garden has structure and height the effect will be unsatisfactory. Few of the plants described in this chapter flower for more than a couple of months, some will be bare and decidedly unattractive for perhaps a third of the year, and a few of the conifers and hedging plants are functional rather than attractive. Yet these are the plants that will create the form and texture of the garden, the backdrop on which to paint the more brilliant and long-lasting displays.

That is not to say that the plants suggested here are dull. Some of the variegated evergreens are beautiful throughout the year; others, like lilacs and some roses, are breathtakingly spectacular for those weeks of glory when they are at their best.

If you get the backbone

plants right, your garden will look interesting and healthy at any time of the year . . . and the more colourful but transient displays from bulbs, bedding and border plants will look that much better for being in an established setting.

GOOD ASSOCIATIONS

Descriptive lists of plants must inevitably form a large part of any book that sets out to suggest plants for problem places. We all want to know what is likely to grow well; it avoids the costly and frustrating failures that come from learning by one's own mistakes. But no matter how good the individual plants, it is how they fit into the garden that really matters. I always get an uplift when I unexpectedly encounter a plant combination or association that really works: the sum is often so much more than the individual constituents. It's why botanic gardens, though always interesting, are frequently less than satisfying when plants are (for good reasons of research or education) grown simply as living collections, like stamps stuck in an album.

Where possible I have suggested some good companion plants, or practical uses, for many of the plants mentioned in this chapter. It's always tempting to buy a plant just because it looks good or appeals in some other way, and like most people I have often had the problem of deciding where to put a plant after I've bought it. So although I may not always practise what I preach, it does make sense to visualize any plant in the garden, in the right association, *before* you buy. The permutations are infinite, but some of the suggestions might appeal as they are, or help to trigger thoughts of an even better plant combination.

PREPARATION AND PLANTING

The principles of good planting have already been described on page 26, but it's always worth reiterating the importance of good ground preparation for trees and shrubs. It really is the only opportunity you'll have to alter the structure fundamentally. Feeding and mulching in subsequent years will help of course, but if you don't break up a solid chalk subsoil *before* you plant, you can't do it afterwards.

The vast majority of trees and shrubs are now sold in

containers anyway, but if you order from mail-order nurseries you will probably receive bare-root plants. You may have no option if you want something unusual that isn't obtainable from local garden centres, but where there is a choice it's especially worthwhile buying plants in pots or other containers if you are planning on an alkaline soil. At least the plants have a root-ball already in suitable compost, which may help to sustain them in the less hospitable ground in your garden during the early months of establishment.

There are two sound rules to follow when planting container-grown plants: gently tease out a few of the larger roots that are wrapping themselves around inside the pot, and bury the root-ball deep enough to be able to cover the top with a couple of centimetres (about an inch) of your own soil.

Teasing out a few roots to spread out in the planting hole reduces the risk of the roots remaining in a tight ball instead of exploring out and down. Covering the root-ball so that it is not exposed to the air reduces the risk of drying out: the probably peaty compost that the roots are in, and the probably dry, stony soil of the garden, may

One of the deutzia hybrids, 'Roselind'. Deutzias are easy to grow, and thrive in a wide range of soil types.

hinder the transfer of soil moisture from one to the other. And if the top of the root-ball compost is exposed to the air it is more likely to dry out quickly.

The shallower the soil, the more temptation there is to give a young tree a massive stake. Huge stakes that dwarf the young tree are certainly unnecessary (especially if they are not firmly anchored anyway because of the difficulty of inserting posts deeply where the soil overlies solid chalk or hard rock). The stake should not come higher than 5 cm (2 in) below the point at which the lowest branches join the trunk. They can be shorter. The ability of the young tree to flex in the wind can actually strengthen it.

Try to fix stakes on the side of the prevailing wind, so that the tree is not blown against the stake unnecessarily.

TREES TO TRY

No garden is too small for at least one tree, albeit one of the very dwarf forms, and I make no apology for including a few large trees too: if the garden is large, the stately 'landscape' trees are necessary to add a sense of perspective. And if you have the space, many of them will

TREE HEIGHTS

Exact tree heights have not been given. So much depends on soil, site, and the part of the country in which you live, that there will be huge variations in trees of the same type and age from one garden to another.

The rate of growth may also affect your choice. Some that are eventually large may be slow-growing and will not out- grow their welcome in your lifetime; others, such as the birches, are quick-growing and will reach close to their ultimate size in a decade or so.

But relative heights are a useful guide, and where the text refers to size, these are the likely ultimate heights in average conditions:

Small 3-10m (10-30ft)
Medium 10-20m (30-60ft)
Large Over 20m (60ft)

---

certainly make superb specimen trees.

It's always worth trying to include a few acers. The common sycamore (A. pseudoplatanus) will grow on alkaline soils, but I would only consider the species itself for an exposed position where something tough is needed. For a prominent position one of the more decorative acers such as 'Brilliantissimum' is a better choice. Although uninspiring for most of the summer, this small tree is a real stunner when it comes into leaf. The leaves open shrimp pink, then take on bronze tints before turning greenish. It's a slow-grower that will take years to become a large tree.

A. cappadocicum, medium to large, has typical lobed sycamore leaves, but they turn a lovely golden yellow in autumn. The variety 'Aureum' is a more attractive tree because it has golden foliage during the summer too.

Of the Norway maples (A. platanoides), 'Drummondii' is one of the most striking, with its white-margined leaves. But you'll have to watch for shoots reverting to green foliage, and cut them out before they begin to dominate the tree. Try 'Crimson King' if you like purple-leaved trees. 'Drummondii' makes a medium to large tree; 'Crimson King' is usually large.

Most of the paper-bark maples are grown for their attractive bark, but A. griseum is such an attractive, small, shapely tree that it's very much an all-rounder. It's main feature is, however, its peeling orange-brown bark. The autumn colour is another key feature.

Acer negundo, the box elder, can be grown as a medium-sized tree or as a shrub. But choose the variegated 'Elegans' (also known as 'Elegantissima') or 'Variegatum' (sometimes listed as 'Aureovariegatum'). Both are fine variegated foliage plants, but again you must cut out any all-green shoots that start appearing.

Horse chestnuts are more in place in public parks than private gardens, but they will grow well on alkaline soils and there are a few choice kinds that make smaller trees than the usual *Aesculus hippocastanum*. The red horse chestnut, *A. x carnea* is a medium-sized tree worth considering for a large garden, or choose the even more compact 'Briotii'. Perhaps the best horse chestnut for a chalky soil is *A. indica,* which has narrow white 'candles', flushed pink and yellow, in early and mid summer. It makes a medium-sized tree.

The strawberry trees *(Arbutus)* sometimes have strawberry-like fruits, but the feature that you can depend on with these small to medium trees is the wonderful brown or cinnamon-red bark. *A. x andrachnoides* is one of the most magnificent, but you'll have to be patient as it's a slow-grower.

The birches inevitably put in an appearance in almost any book that mentions trees. They are so easy, so quick, and so versatile. They can be beautiful too. The silver birch *(Betula pendula)* is a medium to large tree that will find a foothold almost anywhere, and it's well worth growing for its silvery bark and graceful habit. There are birches with even better barks: try *B. ermanii* or *B. papyrifera*. Both make medium to large trees. For a weeping tree of modest size, Young's weeping birch *(B. pendula* 'Youngii') is one of the best. It will remain a small tree.

The Judas tree *(Cercis siliquastrum)* is a spectacular sight in late spring with its clusters of purplish-pink pea-type flowers on naked branches. On mature trees clusters of flowers will even sprout directly from the trunk. Sadly it's a slow-grower, but it will eventually make a rounded, bushy, small tree.

Hawthorns *(Crataegus)* will tolerate alkaline soils, but growth may be restricted if the soil is also dry and impoverished. As these are usually grown as small trees anyway, you may want to take the risk. For flowers the double red *C. oxyacantha* 'Paul's Scarlet' (also 'Cocci-

nea Plena') is one of the most striking, but for a long-lasting display of berries try *C. x lavallei* (also sold as *C. carrierei*). All are small trees.

For a talking-point, plant the pocket-handkerchief tree *(Davidia involucrata)*, but do it soon as it takes years to reach flowering size. The large white bracts hang from the tree like white handkerchiefs. It eventually makes a medium-sized tree.

Laburnums would be highly prized trees if they were rare, but because they are so commonplace we are inclined to take them for granted. They are dull, uninspiring, small trees for the rest of the year, but in early summer the long yellow chains are among the most spectacular of all tree flowers. It's also an easy tree to train over arches to form a yellow 'tunnel' of cascading flowers. I also like to see a vigorous clematis, such as the white *C. montana* and the pink *C. montana rubens* trained through its branches. Training is not an apt word – you only need to plant it where the stems can grow up and through the tree. The clematis will flower at the same time as the laburnum: a wonderful combination.

As laburnum seeds are poisonous, it makes sense to grow 'Vossii' – (one of the best anyway), as it sets few seeds.

I include the crab apples *(Malus)* with some reservation. They are among the most useful multi-merit trees (blossom, fruit, and often good autumn colour), but none of the specimens that I've really admired have been on limy soils. As they are so closely related to the culinary apple, which it is generally agreed does not do well on chalky soils, this comes as no surprise. Yet the crab apples are frequently recommended for limy soils in books and catalogues – I suspect it is because other soil and environmental factors have a role almost as important as the pH. They are such wonderful plants that it is probably worth trying them, but prepare the soil very well first.

A few of my favourite crab apples are 'John Downie' (white flowers, scarlet and yellow fruit), *M. floribunda* (a mass of pink-flushed white blossom), and *M. tschonoskii* (a narrow, upright tree with spectacular autumn colour – which has given it the common name of bonfire tree). All small trees, though *M. tschonoskii* may eventually grow into a medium-sized tree.

If I have some reservations about including *Malus*, I have

The spindle tree, Euonymus europaeus, thrives on chalky soils. This is 'Red Cascade', perhaps the finest form to grow for the red fruits.

none about *Prunus*. Granted, the cherry laurel *(Prunus laurocerasus)* can become chlorotic on shallow chalk soils, but you can use *P. lusitanica,* the Portugal laurel, instead. It makes a small to medium tree.

There are so many good *Prunus* species and varieties that any mentioned must be a short and arbitrary list from a much wider range of possibilities. One of the least spectacular from a distance, but always worth growing because it will flower intermittently all winter, is *P. subhirtella autumnalis.* The species is white, but there's also a pink form. Both make small trees.

Try to find space for the small *P. x amygdalo-persica* and its richer pink form 'Pollardii', hybrids between the peach and the almond. For a contrast in flower shape and form there's the bird cherry *(P. padus),* with white racemes. But choose the variety 'Grandiflora' (also sold as 'Watereri'), which has better flowers. It makes a small to medium-sized tree.

There are all the Japanese cherries as well as a mass of species and other hybrids that are well worth growing. It's all a matter of taste . . . I happen to have a sneaking admiration for 'Kanzan' with its bold pink double flowers, generally on rather stiff, upward-angled branches.

One of the best purple-leaved small trees is *P. cerasifera* 'Pissardii' (also known as 'Atropurpurea'). It has the bonus of white flowers in early spring – not particularly bright but useful for cutting for indoor decoration. Its real worth lies in the purple foliage. 'Nigra' is very similar, but with slightly darker leaves and pinkish flowers.

The pear family does not generally do well on shallow chalk soils, but on deeper alkaline soils and where the ground is well prepared, it's worth trying the popular weeping willow-leaved pear, *Pyrus salicifolia* 'Pendula'. It's one of the best small weeping trees, and its silvery-grey foliage makes it a real feature as a specimen tree.

Robinias are graceful trees that will usually tolerate alkaline soils. One of the most graceful is *R. pseudoacacia*, which has the merit of growing quickly yet not usually outgrowing its welcome. 'Frisia' is a golden form that is extremely attractive even from a distance. It makes a small to medium tree, retains its good colour for the whole season, and it has become a popular tree everywhere. Its growth may be restricted on very alkaline soils, but it is such an outstanding tree that it's worth trying.

The *Sorbus* provide another invaluable group of trees to try. The whitebeams *(S. aria* and its varieties) and the Swedish whitebeam *(S. intermedia)* are small to medium trees that do well on chalk. They have leaves that are downy and grey beneath, producing a delightful silvery effect in the wind. There are also clusters of white flowers in spring and red or orange berries in autumn, but they are grown mainly for foliage effect.

The mountain ash *(S. aucuparia)* and its varieties will also put in a good performance, though they tend to be shorter lived than the whitebeams on shallow chalk soils. Apart from masses of red berries (some hybrids and other species have orange, red, pink, yellow, and white berries), there is usually good autumn colour. They are small or medium trees. *S. vilmorinii* is a good species to try: it is a small tree with fern-like leaves and long-lasting berries that start red and eventually turn pink and almost white. Red-berried forms usually have the fruit stripped by birds very early, but the yellow-berried kinds tend to be less affected by this problem. Another excellent sorbus, is *S.* 'Joseph Rock' which has clusters of yellow berries on striking red stalks. The berries later turn amber and persist late into winter. It has an upright habit and the foliage takes on brilliant autumn tints.

OTHER USEFUL TREES FOR LIMY SOILS

- Ailanthus altissima (tree of heaven – large)
- Alnus cordata (Italian alder – medium to large)
- Amelanchier (shad bush – small)
- Fagus sylvatica (beech – large)
- Fraxinus excelsior (common ash – large)
- Fraxinus ornus (manna ash – medium)
- Juglans (walnut – large)
- Koelreuteria paniculata (golden rain tree – small)
- Liriodendron tulipifera (tulip tree – large)
- Morus (mulberry – small to medium)
- Populus alba (white poplar – large)
- Quercus cerris (Turkey oak – large)
- Quercus ilex (evergreen oak – large)
- Tilia (lime – medium to large)

A SHORTLIST OF SHRUBS

Despite the many shrubs mentioned in this chapter, it gives only a small percentage of what you could grow. It is to some extent a personal selection, though on the basis of general merit rather than personal preference. To keep the list manageable only representative species and varieties have been mentioned in most cases. Just a handful of lilacs are mentioned, but you can buy more than 30, and they will all thrive on chalk; a personal selection of viburnums has been given, but there are more than 100 species and varieties of viburnum, most of which will do well on chalk. In the case of viburnums there are a few that are intolerant of lime, but this has been noted where relevant on page 67.

Wherever possible, important exceptions to the lime tolerance within a group of plants is mentioned, and unless otherwise stated it can be assumed that most other species or varieties are also lime-tolerant.

Bear in mind that the type and depth of the soil, as well as the pH, will affect which plants will do well and which will languish.

Despite a natural reluctance to predict heights (so much depends on soil and site, as well age), an indication of size has been given at the end of each entry. *Large* means over 3 m (10 ft), *Medium* 1.5-3 m (5-10 ft), *Small* 1-1.5 m (3-5 ft), and *Dwarf* 30-60 cm (1-2 ft). These are likely heights after ten years, in average conditions some quick-growing shrubs will reach their height more quickly.

ABELIA

You are quite likely to walk by an abelia and almost miss it if you are talking or otherwise preoccupied. They don't grab attention in the way that say a rhododendron or forsythia does. Despite that they are well worth getting to know, not least because some of them flower over such a long period – from early summer to mid autumn in the case of *A. x grandiflora,* and they are semi-evergreen.

The pink-tinged white flowers in small clusters at the ends of leafy branches are slightly fragrant (at least in *A. x grandiflora* and *A. triflora,* two of the most dependable species). Some of the other species are fairly tender. *A. x grandiflora* with white, pink tinted flowers in summer and autumn makes a small to medium-sized shrub. *A. triflora,* with white and pink flowers in early summer, becomes a large shrub.

Abelias are useful for the front of a mixed shrub border, where their smaller flowers and fragrance can be appreciated from a path or lawn.

AMELANCHIER
Snowy mespilus
There's confusion in the naming and distribution of the snowy mespilus: *A. canadensis, A. laevis* and *A. lamarckii* are all similar, and often one gets sold as another. This time it doesn't really matter to the gardener because they are all well worth having.

The amelanchiers are true multi-merit shrubs, which puts them high on my list. The display starts in mid or late spring, when the bushes are covered with a snowy mass of white starry flowers. Although the individual flowers are fairly small, this is not a shrub that will be overlooked – it will command attention when in flower.

In early summer, there may be a bonus of sweet-tasting round, black berries. Don't bank on this feature, however; in many years, and on young plants, there won't be enough fruit to make such a vivid impression.

There will be no doubt about its impact in autumn, however, when the foliage takes on wonderful autumn colours.

You might find these amelanchiers listed in some books as trees. They can be grown on a single main stem as a small tree, but more usually they are many-branched and make large shrubs instead.

Try planting an amelanchier as a specimen plant, or massed in a group, where they can be viewed against a dark background such as a shady wall. But if possible keep the plants themselves in the sun.

ARUNDINARIA
Bamboo
These bamboos will usually do well over chalk provided there is a reasonable depth of soil. One of the best and most elegant bamboos, *A. nitida* is useful for partial shade.

Try it as a specimen plant, or even as a screen . . . but bear in mind that it can grow up to 3 m (10 ft) or more.

AUCUBA
Spotted laurel
Perhaps because they will grow almost anywhere, even in shade, the aucubas, or spotted laurels, are often dismissed as rather uninteresting plants. If you choose the plain green form, and a male into the bargain, it has to be admitted that you'll have a dull plant. But there are some super variegated varieties of *Aucuba japonica,* such as 'Crotonifolia' and 'Variegata'

(the latter is a female and therefore has red berries too).

Try the aucubas, which make medium-sized shrubs, for difficult shady places.

BERBERIS
Barberries

You could have a whole border of berberis and have something of interest for most of the year. There are evergreen as well as deciduous kinds, varieties with golden, purple, and variegated foliage, and species with eye-catching flowers, autumn tints, and beautiful berries. There are many to choose from, and for reasons of space only a handful are mentioned here.

Among the evergreens, B. darwinii is my favourite. The dark green foliage is like small holly leaves. These make a wonderful background for the masses of bright orange flowers in spring. There's also a bonus of blue berries later.

B. stenophylla is another outstanding evergreen, covered with yellow flowers in mid spring. It has a more straggly habit than the previous species, but it makes an impenetrable flowering hedge.

Among the deciduous species, B. thunbergii is justifiably one of the most popular, although it may become chlorotic on very poor alkaline soils. It is usually grown in the form atropurpurea. If you want a dwarfer plant 'Atropurpurea Nana' is ideal.

There are many interesting varieties of B. thunbergii, including narrow, upright forms, and variegated types such as 'Rose Glow'.

For masses of berries in late summer, and brilliant autumn foliage colour, try B. wilsoniae. It seldom grows more than 1 m (3 ft) so it should be possible to find room for it.

B. darwinii will make a large shrub, but the others mentioned will make only small to medium-sized shrubs, and therefore B. darwinii will make a superb specimen shrub in a lawn, while most of the others are best in a mixed shrub border. Try some of the purple berberis in association with some of the variegated euonymus, or in front of the golden Robinia pseudoacacia 'Frisia'.

BUDDLEIA
Butterfly bush

The most popular of the buddleias, the aptly-named butterfly bush (B. davidii), is such a determined grower that it can be found holding on to life as a self-sown seedling on old walls, or even growing in the small amount of soil that has accumulated in the neglected gutters of old buildings. Clearly that's the sort of stamina that makes it an ideal plant for even the most difficult chalk soils.

If regular spring pruning is neglected, the plants become straggly and rather ungainly, but by cutting them hard back in early spring it's possible to create compact and shapely bushes. The flowers form at the end of arching shoots in mid and late summer. There are several named varieties, in colours ranging from white through shades of blue and lilac to red-purple. Even if the flowers were not attractive, the plant would still be worth growing for the butterflies that it attracts.

B. davidii will make a medium to large shrub. *B. alternifolia* is a large shrub that's worth growing for its cascading sprays of lavender-blue flowers in summer.

Buddleias are useful for the back of a mixed border, or towards the front of a shrub border (where the arching flower sprays can cascade forward over the lawn above mower height).

CALLICARPA

Although it can become slightly chlorotic on very thin chalk soils, *C. bodinieri giraldii* is one of those plants that it is always worth trying to incude for its interesting violet fruits. For reasons of pollination, you'll need to grow several plants close together, however, to be sure of a good display of fruits. A medium-sized shrub with lilac flowers in late summer, and good autumn foliage colour.

Callicarpas are not showy plants except when in fruit, so plant towards the front of a shrub border, where all the berries can be seen.

CARYOPTERIS

C. x clandonensis is a dwarf, grey-leaved shrub with blue flowers that looks as at home in the herbaceous border as in a shrub border. The stems are often killed in a severe winter, but new ones will usually spring up again from the base the following season.

Try the variety 'Arthur Simmonds' (or 'Heavenly Blue' if you prefer darker flowers).

Don't be afraid to use this shrub in the mixed or herbaceous border. It looks good in a silver or grey border. In the early spring old dead stems should be cut down close to the ground.

CERATOSTIGMA
Hardy plumbago
C. willmottianum is a pretty dwarf to small semi-evergreen shrub, with blue phlox-like flowers from mid summer and into autumn, when the foliage colours well. In cold winters the stems may be cut back, but new shoots usually appear again in spring.

It is a useful plant to fill in the gap between taller shrubs and the lawn edge, provided the position is sunny.

CHAENOMELES
Japanese quince; japonica
The ornamental quinces can be very straggly plants unless carefully pruned to keep them tidy, but with proper training they are among the very best flowering wall plants. Don't hesitate to try any of the *C. speciosa* or *C. x superba* varieties. There are reds, pinks, and whites.

Grown as free-standing shrubs in a border, the chaenomeles can look untidy and disappointing. It's well worth the trouble of training them as wall plants.

CHIMONANTHUS PRAECOX
Winter sweet
Sometimes sold under its old name of *C. fragrans*, the winter sweet is one of the best winter-flowering shrubs for chalk soils. The waxy-looking flowers are yellow-stained purple at the centre. They are not conspicuous from a distance on the bare stems in winter, but they are fascinating flowers when viewed closely . . . and deliciously fragrant—especially when pinched.

Definitely one to grow if at all possible, but it will need a very warm position (it does especially well against a sunny wall), and you will have to be patient because young plants don't flower well.

Site this medium-sized shrub near a path that you use a lot, perhaps against a wall close to the door.

CHOISYA TERNATA
Mexican orange blossom
Although I would hesitate to plant this in a very cold or exposed area, it's a really super evergreen. It takes its common name of Mexican orange blossom from the fragrance of the white flowers, which appear in late spring and intermittently throughout the summer. The leaves are also fragrant when crushed.

Although a candidate for the shrub border, it makes a more striking shrub grown as a specimen, perhaps flanking steps, or in a bed by the door.

CISTUS
Sun rose
The sun roses revel in a dry, sunny position. There are several good species and hybrids, making small or medium-sized evergreen shrubs, but a severe winter will take its toll of most of them.

Among the hardiest are *C. x corbariensis*, crimson in bud, opening white; *C. laurifolius*, white with yellow centre; *C. populifolius*, white petals with a yellow base. 'Silver Pink' is the lovely shade described by its name. There are many others if you really don't mind taking more of a risk with the winter losses.

Two invaluable ground covers—ivy and Euonymus *'Emerald 'n' Gold', both easily grown in sun or partial shade (the ivy can even be grown in heavy shade).*

These are super plants for a dry, sunny bank.

CORNUS
Dogwood
It's the dogwoods (*C. alba* and *C. stolonifera*) that are particularly useful shrubs – especially for winter interest. The various varieties of *C. alba* are grown largely for their red stems in winter; *C. stolonifera* 'Flaviramea' for its yellow-green shoots. All are best cut down almost to ground level in spring (annually or every-other year) to stimulate the production of plenty of young shoots.

I like multi-merit plants, and for that reason I prefer to grow 'Elegantissima' and 'Spaethii' in preference to the species *C. alba* or its other varieties. Both are variegated, the first splashed silver, the second gold.

If you have room for only one plant, choose one of the two variegated varieties suggested; the winter display won't be spectacular, but they are excellent shrubs for summer interest. For winter effect, they need to be massed, with perhaps a large group of the yellowish *C. stolonifera* 'Flaviramea' in front of groups of red-stemmed dogwoods. Even more interest can be added by using a bright evergreen groundcover between the plants, such as the gold and green *Euonymus fortunei* 'Emerald 'n' Gold'.

COTINUS COGGYGRIA
Smoke bush
This plant may still be found as *Rhus cotinus*, but its common name of smoke bush is the most descriptive. The inflorescences create a haze-like cloud effect above the plant in early and mid summer, persisting and turning a smoke-grey by late summer. Good autumn tints are a bonus. There are purple-leaved forms such as 'Royal Purple' and 'Notcutt's Variety'.

A good all-round shrub, either in a mixed or shrub border or as a specimen plant in a lawn. The purple-leaved forms are best as isolated specimens, otherwise the foliage-effect tends to be lost against the dark greens of other shrubs.

COTONEASTER
This is an important group of plants for alkaline soils, because they range from prostrate carpeters to large shrubs and small trees. They have small pink or white flowers in summer, but most are grown for their long-lasting berries.

Any shortlist of cotoneasters must be arbitrary in its selection, and there are many other good ones.

For groundcover, try *C. conspicuus* 'Decorus', a semi-evergreen that is excellent for covering banks. *C. horizontalis* will also spread along the ground as a carpeter, but it is equally happy growing upwards if planted against a wall. Apart from the excellent berrying capacity of this plant, it has a brief week or two of really rich autumn colour. 'Variegatus' is a variety with cream-variegated leaves, which are suffused red in autumn.

C. simonsii is a semi-evergreen sometimes used for hedges. It is not, however, a particularly neat or outstanding shrub in other ways.

Where there's space, perhaps towards the back of a large border, or even as isolated specimens in a large lawn, try some of the large upright kinds. 'Cornubia' is one to try if you want to see branches really laden with big berries.

A particular favourite of mine for a small garden is *C.* 'Hybridus Pendulus', which when grown on a stem makes a small weeping tree with a waterfall of red berries in autumn. A superb small specimen tree in the lawn for a small garden. But make sure you get one trained as a tree form when you buy, as you can also obtain it as a low-growing carpeting plant.

DAPHNE
On shallow chalk soils one of the very best daphnes, *D. mezereum,* can become chlorotic, but on deeper soils it often puts on a good show. Its very fragrant purple-red flowers appear on naked stems in late winter and early spring. 'Alba' is a white form.

D. cneorum, the garland flower, can be difficult to establish, but is worth the effort because the usually pink flowers in late spring have such a delightful fragrance.

Both these, and most of the other species, are small shrubs. Although the two mentioned are hardy, some of the other species may need shelter or protection.

DEUTZIA
There are several good deutzias, making small or medium-sized shrubs that flower in early and mid summer. Although the individual pink or white flowers are small and unexciting, the bushes are eye-catching when covered in bloom. There are single and double forms.

To ensure a shapely bush, prune back shoots after they have flowered, and remove old, unproductive wood.

Because deutzias are uninteresting outside their flowering season, they are best planted at the front of a shrub border, preferably near shrubs that will flower at different times, such as the late-flowering hibiscus.

ELAEAGNUS
E. pungens 'Maculata' is common but no less meritorious for that. It's one of my

favourite shrubs. The gold and green evergreen leaves look good at any time of year, but are especially striking in winter sunshine. Try using it as a focal point, perhaps against a background of either deciduous or dark-leaved evergreen shrubs.

E. x ebbingei is less spectacular, but it's useful as a fast-growing screen and for coastal planting. It has silvery foliage and unspectacular but fragrant flowers in late summer.

Both make medium to large shrubs.

ERICA
Heath; heather
Heaths and heathers are associated with acid soils, but there are a few that will tolerate alkaline soils (but not shallow chalky ground). Fortunately *E. carnea*, now increasingly sold under the name *E. herbacea*, is one of them. Flowering in winter, and with lots of varieties, it's one of the most useful.

Other ericas that can be considered for alkaline (but not shallow chalk) soils are *E. x darleyensis* and *E. mediterranea*.

ESCALLONIA
Escallonias are of borderline hardiness in cold areas in a bad winter, but they are worth trying in milder areas. They are good evergreens for coastal areas, and 'Red Hedger' is a particularly good choice for a small hedge.

Most species and varieties have red or pink flowers, and the shrubs range from small to large in size (depending on species and variety).

Some varieties and species are likely to do better than others. 'Iveyi' and 'Langleyensis' are two of the most dependable.

Escallonias do not usually make good border shrubs, and are usually seen at their best as a hedge or a screen.

EUONYMUS
Euonymus are invaluable shrubs, and they have a variety of uses. The plain green *E. japonicus* is one of the best evergreens for hedges in coastal areas, and the variegated kinds such as 'Ovatus Aureus' are good general-purpose evergreens for the shrub border (but need a sunny site).

The spindle (*E. europaeus*) is a shrub that chooses chalky soils as a natural habitat. It makes a multi-stemmed large shrub or a small tree. Its main attraction is the red fruit capsules in autumn. 'Red Cascade' is a selected form that fruits prolifically.

Very different are the forms of *E. fortunei*, most of which will trail as a ground cover or climb a wall or fence if suitably placed. Two of the best-known varieties are 'Emerald Gaiety' (silver and green) and 'Emerald 'n' Gold' (gold and green).

Hibiscus syriacus, *one of the most valuable late-flowering shrubs. This variety is 'Coelestis'.*

FORSYTHIA

The bright yellow forsythia, part of spring everywhere, needs no introduction. Don't dismiss it just because it's commonplace – it's widely grown because it is such a good shrub.

There are delicate species such as *F. suspensa,* and large-flowered varieties such as 'Beatrix Farrand', but one of the finest for sheer show is 'Lynwood'.

Forsythias are useful for bringing early colour to a shrub border. All make medium to large shrubs.

GARRYA

G. elliptica is a superb evergreen, useful for planting in front of a north or east wall, although it is not suitable for very cold areas.

Garryas come into their own in winter, when long catkins cascade off the branches. The male plants have the most impressive catkins, and 'James Roof' is a male form to look out for.

Although they can be planted in a shrub border, they look their most magnificent planted with a wall as a background, in a conspicuous spot where they can be appreciated on a winter's day.

GENISTA

From a distance, *G. aetnensis* looks just like a large yellow broom flowering out of season (it blooms in mid-summer).

The common name is Mount Etna broom. It makes a large shrub or small tree.

Two other very worthwhile genistas are *G. cinerea* (fragrant yellow flowers in early and mid-summer; medium size) and *G. hispanica,* the Spanish gorse (masses of yellow flowers in late spring and early summer; dwarf). The latter is especially good for a dry, sunny bank.

G. lydia is another dwarf eyecatcher with yellow flowers in late spring and early summer.

HEBE

Hebes are unreliable in cold areas, but many do well in milder coastal regions (ironically, although possibly killed by a cold winter, some flower well into winter). If hebes seem to thrive in your area, it's well worth growing some.

Most hebes have bottle-brush-like flowers, unimpressive in some, attractive in others. Many are worth growing for the attractive evergreen mounds that they make.

Just three to try are 'Autumn Glory' (violet flowers in late summer and autumn), 'Midsummer Beauty' (lavender flowers throughout the summer), and *H. x franciscana* 'Variegata' (leaves edged creamy-white).

All those mentioned make small shrubs, and are useful for the front of a shrub or mixed border. *H. x francis-cana* 'Variegata' makes a very attractive edging for beds used for seasonal bedding.

HELIANTHEMUM
Sun rose; rock rose
The *Helianthemum nummu-larium* hybrids, popularly known a sun roses or rock roses, are listed in some books and catalogues under herbaceous plants. They do have woody top growth, so here they are included with the shrubs. Many have attractive greyish foliage, some have double flowers (not, in my opinion, as effective as the singles). Colours include pink, yellow, red and orange.

They are covered with flowers in early summer, and if you trim the plants with shears after flowering you will probably have another flush of flowers in late summer. Unfortunately, they tend to become straggly and die out after a few years, so it's worth taking cuttings regularly to replace the plants.

The helianthemums look good in gravel gardens, large rock gardens, or edging herbaceous borders. But they are at their most spectacular massed on a sunny bank. Don't be afraid to try them with some of the vigorous and bright early summer rock plants such as the yellow *Alyssum saxatile* or purple aubrieta. They can look stunning growing together in a rock garden or on a sunny slope.

HIBISCUS
For anyone who believes in the importance of spreading the flowering season in the shrub border over as long a period as possible, the varieties of *H. syriacus* are invaluable. The large mallow-shaped flowers appear between late summer and mid autumn.

Colours include pink, purple, red, blue, and white, some blotched. There are doubles, but the singles often have more impact.

They need a hot, sunny position to do well.

HYPERICUM
The rose of Sharon *(H. calycinum)* is often dismissed as a coarse and invasive plant. It's not one to plant in a mixed border or as a single specimen in a shrub border, but it's a really useful plant for ground-cover for difficult positions. It's evergreen, very tough, will grow in sun or shade, and becomes a carpet of yellow when flowering. Use it to clothe a bank that's difficult to cultivate.

For the shrub border, choose 'Hidcote', a superb semi-evergreen small shrub with saucer-shaped yellow flowers from mid-summer to mid-autumn.

Don't be afraid to try other hypericums, many of which are excellent plants.

LAVANDULA
Lavender

There are several good lavenders, and all of them will do well on alkaline soil. The nomenclature has become confused over the years, and you might find the old English lavender under the names *L. angustifolia* or *L. spica*. Although there are white, pink, and other pale shades, the darker colours are much more striking.

Although comparatively short-lived, a lavender hedge is really eye-catching in flower, fragrant, and neat for most of the year. Try it for a low informal hedge, or use individual plants to punctuate a herb garden.

MAGNOLIA

Magnolias are especially popular large shrubs or small trees. The most popular, *M. x soulangiana*, won't do well on chalky soils. Nor will many other species. Those that can be tried with a good chance of success include *M. x highdownensis* and *M. wilsonii* (both have pendulous white flowers), *M. kobus* (white flowers), and *M. x loebneri* (white or pink flowers). If I had to choose just one it would be *M. x loebneri* 'Leonard Messel'.

A word of warning for the impatient: magnolias may take years to start flowering. Sometimes it can take more than 10 years for some of them to start blooming.

MAHONIA

Mahonias are dependable border shrubs, with glossy evergreen leaves that may take on purplish-red colouring in winter. All have yellow flowers, which show up well against the dark green foliage.

M. japonica has fragrant lemon-yellow flowers in the winter months. *M.* 'Charity' is a striking shrub with slightly fragrant, deep yellow flowers in late autumn and early winter.

Mahonias are useful in shrub or mixed borders, but can also make an attractive specimen plant in a lawn. Those mentioned make medium-sized shrubs.

OLEARIA
Daisy bush

The common name of daisy bush describes these shrubs well: they are covered with white daisy-type flowers in summer. You may find several species in garden centres, but *O. x haastii* is one of the toughest. It makes a small, rounded shrub, and can be used for a hedge.

Many olearias are of borderline hardiness in all but the mildest areas.

X OSMAREA

X O. 'Burkwoodii' is a bigeneric hybrid between *Osmanthus delavayi* and *Phillyrea decora*. It is a first-rate medium-sized evergreen

Philadelphus x lemoinei, *one of the most fragrant summer-flowering shrubs.*

shrub, with fragrant white flowers in mid or late spring.

PAEONIA
Tree peony

The tree peonies are really imposing plants. The foliage of some of them, such as *P. lutea,* is very decorative even when the plants are not in flower. It is, of course, the big, bold blooms that are the main attraction. The hybrids of *P. suffrutricosa* are among the most magnificent. These medium to large shrubs have single or double flowers in shades of red, pink, and white. For a yellow, try *P. lutea ludlowii.*

It is worth protecting young growth from late frosts, which may damage the shoots of some tree peonies.

Although good candidates for a shrub border, don't be afraid to use them to add height and boldness to a mixed border too.

PHILADELPHUS
Mock orange

Commonly called mock orange, they are generally very fragrant, and although most have white flowers they are nevertheless bold and cheerful shrubs in flower. Keep to the scented varieties, and for impact from a distance to singles.

Just three good ones are 'Beauclerk' (medium-sized shrub, milk-white flowers with cerise base), 'Belle Etoile' (small to medium size, white flushed maroon at centre), and 'Avalanche' (small, white). If you want to try a double, 'Virginal' is certainly one of the best.

POTENTILLA
Shrubby potentilla

The shrubby potentillas make dwarf to small shrubs that flower from early summer and right into autumn. Varieties and hybrids of *P. fruticosa* are among the best. Most bloom prolifically with single cream, yellow, or orange flowers. 'Red Ace' is red and 'Tangerine' becomes a strong rusty-orange if grown in the shade.

PYRACANTHA
Firethorn

Pyracanthas can be grown as free-standing shrubs, but they are at their most magnificent when well trained as wall shrubs. There are species and varieties with red, orange, and yellow berries. It's best not to grow pyracanthas where fireblight is a disease of fruit trees, as it can also affect pyracanthas. 'Orange Glow' is fairly disease-resistant and it holds its orange-red fruits well into winter.

RIBES
Flowering currant

The flowering currant, *Ribes sanguineum* and its varieties, is a popular spring-flowering shrub. The flower clusters range from pink to red, depending on variety. Unfortunately flowering currants tend to look boring for the rest of the year, but 'Brocklebankii' is a smaller shrub with very attractive yellow leaves. This one is attractive all summer provided it is not in full sun (which tends to scorch the leaves).

ROSA
Rose
There are so many roses, and personal preferences and prejudices play such an important part, that I make no shortlist. Just a plea to try some of the climbers through suitable trees – perhaps 'Wedding Day' through a spring-flowering prunus. This richly scented creamy-white rose can bring a tree to life with a second flush of flowers just as you begin to think the tree is starting to look boring. By coincidence, this rose was actually raised in a chalk garden.

SAROCOCCA
Christmas box
The Christmas box is a plant that you'll probably pass by without giving it a glance for most of the year ... but it will bring a touch of fragrance to the garden in late winter. The species usually grown is *S. humilis* which grows to about 60 cm (2 ft).

This is a useful evergreen for cutting, so give it a try – it will make up for summer drabness with winter interest.

SPARTIUM JUNCEUM
Spanish broom
The Spanish broom is especially good as a coastal plant, but well worth considering for any hot, dry spot. It's covered with yellow flowers in summer and into early autumn. By the coast it may be wind-pruned to keep it shapely, elsewhere it will have to be trimmed back in spring to avoid it becoming a gawky shape.

SYRINGA
Lilac
The lilacs really thrive on alkaline soils – the British National Collection is located on a chalky hillside.

The most popular lilacs are the varieties of *S. vulgaris*, and there are singles and doubles, in blue, lilac, pink, purple, carmine, red, white, and cream ... and all wonderfully fragrant. The trouble with all of them is the natural tendency to make tall leggy plants unless carefully pruned. Remove old flowered shoots immediately after the flowers are over, and shorten very strong shoots in summer if necessary to keep the bush compact and shapely.

Great though the varieties of *S. vulgaris* are, especially as cut flowers, I prefer the more graceful species such as *S. x persica* (the Persian lilac),

and *S. x prestoniae* varieties. There are lots more to try, and all of them should do well, even on very alkaline soils. All lilacs should be well and generously mulched each year.

TAMARIX
Tamarisk

The tamarisks are associated with coastal areas, but they will thrive inland too. Although they will tolerate alkaline soils, don't expect them to do well on shallow chalk soils.

Two of the best tamarisks are *T. pentandra* 'Rubra' and *T. tetrandra*. The first has pink flowers in late summer and early autumn, the second in late spring or early summer.

VIBURNUM

There are so many viburnums that any shortlist is likely to leave out good plants, and all of them should do well on chalk.

For summer interest, it's difficult to ignore *V. plicatum* with its big head of white flowers.

'Mariesii' is a variety with especially attractive tiered branches. 'Rowallane' is similar but has the bonus of a particularly heavy crop of red berries in autumn.

Worth growing for its lush red autumn berries is the Guelder rose, *Viburnum opulus;* for yellow berries try the variety 'Xanthocarpum'.

I never cease to be amazed by the determination of the laurustinus *(V. tinus)* to flower all winter. It can be seen starting to bloom before autumn is out, and it may still be blooming as the spring flowers appear. Add to that its good, tidy and compact shape, and useful evergreen foliage, and you have a plant worth having. It makes a medium to large shrub, suitable for growing as a specimen plant or in the shrub border. The flowers on the species are basically white, but look for 'Eve Price' (a good form with pink flowers and red buds).

There are other winter-flowering viburnums, some very fragrant, and mention has to be made of *V. x bodnantense*, especially the varieties 'Dawn' and 'Deben'. The small clusters of white or pink flowers are produced from mid-autumn onwards, and throughout the winter in mild spells. Well worth growing to cut for winter decoration indoors, but I find that frost damage generally spoils the flowers outdoors. And I personally don't find the sparse look of this deciduous shrub attractive.

Although not common plants, there are a few species that do not tolerate lime, particularly *V. cassinoides*, *V. corylifolium*, *V. dentatum*, *V. furcatum*, and *V. nudum*.

Pyracantha *'Mojave'*. *The pyracanthas are excellent wall shrubs, and this variety is one of the most disease-resistant.*

CLIMBERS

Climbers are useful in any garden, but especially so in a small garden where space is at a premium. The use of vertical space not only enables more plants to be grown, but it also helps to avoid bare walls and fences. And by growing suitable climbers, such as clematis and honeysuckles, through other plants it's possible to extend the period of interest in a given area. Alkaline soils are no handicap: almost all the most beautiful climbers will thrive. And although the list of genera included here is small, the actual choice of varieties is vast. There are dozens of excellent clematis, even more good roses, and a vast collection of ivies (hederas) from which to choose.

ACTINIDIA KOLOMIKTA
Kolomikta vine
It's not worth growing this on a shallow chalk soil, but on deeper alkaline loams it should do well. Although the leaf variegation may be lost as the season progresses, especially in poor light, it is a real talking-point at its best.

In good conditions the green leaves are boldly splashed white and overlaid with patches of pink. Best against a south or west facing wall, in full sun.

Grows to about 3.5 m (12 ft).

AKEBIA QUINATA
This is a plant it's easy to walk past, even when in flower, yet I never cease to be fascinated by it. This semi-evergreen has racemes of fragrant red-purple flowers in mid-spring which some gardeners say smell of chocolate; it is certainly a distinctive fragrance.

You will sometimes see it described in books and catalogues as a rampant climber with purple sausage-shaped fruits. In cool climates such as Britain, my experience has been that it is far from rampant, and I have yet to see the fruits (a mild spring and a long, hot summer are required for the fruits to be a feature). Nevertheless it is a very interesting plant.

Will grow to about 10 m (30 ft) if conditions suit it, but often no more than 3 m (10 ft).

CLEMATIS
Clematis can do very well on chalk, especially if the roots are in shade and the flowers in the sun. There are too many kinds to describe here, and for a choice of large-flowered hybrids it's best to consult a specialist catalogue. There are, however, a few species that have to be mentioned.

The ubiquitous *C. montana* is ideal for growing along a

fence or up through a tree such as a laburnum or a tall shrub like a lilac. The species itself is white, but *rubens* is pink, and much the more attractive plant to my mind. There are varieties to be found with even better colour, such as 'Tetrarose'.

C. montana will reach more than 9 m (30 ft) given suitable support, but it will also confine itself to a fence of only 1.2 m (4 ft) by growing horizontally.

Try to find somewhere for the more delicate-looking *C. macropetala* ('Markham's Pink' is a good form) which grows to about 3 m (10 ft) if given a suitable support. There are many more interesting clematis, such as *C. orientalis,* with its nodding yellow bells in late summer and early autumn, followed by silky seed heads. *C. tangutica* is perhaps an even better yellow-flowered clematis for poor chalky soils, and is useful for clothing walls, fences, and also banks. Both *C. orientalis* and *C. tangutica* will reach about 4.5-6 m (15-20 ft).

HEDERA
Ivy
The ivies are useful for ground-cover or for clothing a wall or the trunk of a tree. My favourite is the large-leaved *H. colchica* 'Dentata Variegata', with the leaves shading from green to grey and splashed creamy-white. This is ideal for growing round a porch or pergola, but for covering a wall you need the varieties of *H. helix,* the common ivy.

There is much variation in leaf shape and size, as well as colour and variegation. There are plenty from which to choose, but bear in mind that some of the variegated kinds are likely to be much slower in growth than are the green varieties.

H. colchica can reach 6 m (20 ft) or more, *H. helix* three or four times that height. Equally, they will grow along the ground, so don't be afraid to try them because of their theoretical ultimate size.

LONICERA
Honeysuckle
There are many different honeysuckles, including evergreen and semi-evergreen kinds. But for sheer flower power and fragrance don't be sidetracked from growing the common *Lonicera periclymenum* in its form 'Belgica' (late spring and early summer) and 'Serotina' (mid-summer to early autumn). Both may reach 4.5-6 m (15-20 ft) if there is a suitable support.

PARTHENOCISSUS
I often think what a pity it is that these are not evergreen climbers, they cover a high, bare wall so effectively when in leaf. But of course we would then miss the brief but wonderful fireworks as they turn

brilliant orange and scarlet before the leaves fall in autumn.

Two species are sometimes confused, but both are fine plants: *P. quinquefolia* (the Virginia creeper), and *P. tricuspidata* (the Boston ivy). They will grow to 15 m (50 ft) or more.

These two plants will cover even the largest wall, but for a shady wall of more modest size (up to about 9 m (30 ft)) try *P. henryana,* which has silvery-white variegation all summer . . . and still rich autumn colours too. It's best grown in shade or partial shade rather than full sun in order to achieve the most striking variegation.

POLYGONUM BALDSCHUANICUM
Russian vine

The Russian vine, or mile-a-minute vine, isn't especially pretty, but it's quick and it will cover all kinds of unsightly objects, from an oil storage tank to an old shed. The foamy sprays of white flowers are not unattractive and last for a long period ir summer and autumn. It can reach to more than 9 m (30ft), but it does not require a support more than about 2.4 m (8 ft) high.

Right: Viburnum tomentosum *'Mariesii', a beautiful large shrub with tiered branches that can make it a real focal point.*
Opposite: *Clematis thrive on alkaline soils, and 'Nelly Moser' is one of the most striking hybrids.*

CONIFERS

Conifers are invaluable backbone plants because the vast majority of them are evergreen (and there is plenty of variety in foliage colour, including golds and 'blues', and some are variegated). Some do well on alkaline soils – yews and junipers can be found on chalk downland.

I like conifers, and have them in my own garden, but they are often over-planted. Too many will make the outline of the garden look stiff and formal, and it will start to look boring because there are not enough contrasts through the seasons of the year. A combination of coniferous hedges as a backdrop to borders where conifers predominate can become just too much of a good thing.

Although a few examples of conifers that do well on chalk are given below, many others will grow satisfactorily even if they lack the vigour and stature that they would have on better soils. In the case of some dwarf varieties this may not matter. Most perform well on limestone soils.

ABIES
Fir

The firs are generally rather large trees, and therefore only worth considering if you have a large garden. Many of them will do well on alkaline soils, and a few will grow on shallow chalk, particularly *A. cephalonica* and *A. x vilmorinii* both medium to large trees.

CEDRUS
Cedar

Cedars can do very well on shallow soil over chalk, which means you have available some of the very finest specimen trees for a large lawn.

Although the cedar of Lebanon, *C. libani,* is one of the most majestic of all trees when mature, it is one for parks and very large gardens rather than the smaller gardens of today. Choose instead the Atlas cedar (*C. atlantica*) or its varieties, or the deodar (*C. deodara*) which will still make large trees in time but are suitable for a reasonably large garden. The golden forms will make small to medium-sized trees and are suitable for smaller gardens. All lovely trees in time.

CHAMAECYPARIS

The Lawson cypress *C. lawsoniana* has given birth to so many different varieties that there is one for almost every taste. There are literally hundreds of them.

As heights and shapes differ with varieties, you will need to consult a specialist catalogue or book on conifers to decide which are suitable for your garden. But worth considering as a starting point if you become bewildered by them are: 'Allumii' (upright, blue-grey foliage), 'Kilmacurragh' (narrow and columnar, green), and 'Lane' (columnar, golden-yellow). All make medium-sized trees.

CRYPTOMERIA

There are many varieties of *C. japonica*, the only species, but 'Elegans' is a real beauty with feathery foliage that turns reddish in winter. There are compact forms perhaps more suitable for a small space. Although the cryptomerias are sometimes not recommended for chalky soils (certainly they will do better on neutral loams), I have seen some very attractive specimens on alkaline soils. 'Elegans' will make a small tree.

X CUPRESSOCYPARIS

The Leyland cypress *(X C. leylandii)* is one of our fastest-growing trees, and perhaps over-planted. It will make a fast screen, but do remember that its vigour will not stop just when it has reached a convenient height.

If I were planting the Leyland cypress, I would choose 'Castlewellan' (yellow to bronze) or 'Haggerston Grey' (grey-green), to avoid the monotony of too many plants of the green form.

These two will make medium or large trees, but they can also be trimmed to a more moderate size if grown as a hedge.

CUPRESSUS
Cypress
The Monterey cypress, *C. macrocarpa,* has fast initial growth, and in good conditions will make a tree that's too large for a small garden. It is prone to some diseases, and may not do well in cold areas. If you want to try a Monterey cypress, 'Goldcrest' is a pretty golden variety that makes an attractive small tree.

GINKGO
Maidenhair tree
The only species is *G. biloba,* and it is one of the most distinctive of all conifers. The fan-shaped leaves give it the common name of maidenhair tree (the leaves resemble those of the maidenhair fern, but are much larger), and it is one of the few deciduous conifers that we grow. The leaves turn yellow in autumn before falling.

It is slow to grow in the early years, but eventually makes a large and distinctive tree worth planting as a lawn specimen for the future.

JUNIPERUS
Juniper
Junipers do well on chalk, though many have the drawback of slow growth. There

are plenty of good species and varieties, and it is worth looking round a garden centre to see which you like (though as the eventual height and habit also vary considerably with species and variety, make a point of checking on these aspects too).

One of the best true dwarfs (you can even plant it in a sink garden with confidence) is *J. communis* 'Compressa'. The creeping juniper *(J. horizontalis)* will hug the ground and make an impressive ground-cover – the variety 'Bar Harbor' is a good one for this.

A personal favourite is *J. media* 'Pfitzerana Aurea'. It has spreading rather than upright growth, but cannot be called ground-hugging, reaching about 1 m (3 ft). In spring the young spreading shoots are suffused golden-yellow.

METASEQUOIA
Dawn redwood

The dawn redwood *(M. glyptostroboides)* is a vigorous tree unsuitable for small gardens. It will grow on chalk, but prefers moist conditions to dry ones. An imposing, large tree, but only worth considering for the right spot in a big garden.

PICEA
Spruce

Mainly fairly large trees, only a few are suitable for small gardens. One of the most adaptable to difficult soils is the Serbian spruce *(P. omorika)*, a distinctive, but still large tree, with drooping branches that turn upwards at the tips.

PINUS
Pine

Mainly large trees unsuitable for all but the largest gardens, though *P. nigra*, the black pine, will do well on chalk. More modest in size, making a large shrub or small tree, is the mountain pine, *P. mugo*, a plant well worth a place.

TAXUS
Yew

Yews do well on chalk. The common yew *(T. baccata)* can look dull and boring, but there are two excellent varieties: 'Fastigiata' (the Irish yew, making a narrow upright column), and 'Standishii' (similar but golden). Both make small trees. 'Fastigiata Aurea' has a good strong colour but it is slower growing.

THUJA
Arbor-vitae

There are plenty of suitable trees here, some dwarfs (the golden *T. occidentalis* 'Rheingold' for instance) others tall and majestic, like the Western red cedar *(T. plicata)*. You are not likely to want to grow this one as a specimen tree unless you have a very large garden, but it clips so well that you can use for a hedge.

Aubrieta and the yellow Alyssum saxatile, *two of the easiest spring-flowering rock or wall plants to grow, and they thrive on alkaline soils.*

*U*SING ALPINES

There are two ways of looking at alpines in an alkaline garden. If you are simply entranced by the wonderful miniature world of rock plants, you'll want to grow them for their own sake, and will probably want to consider raised beds to extend the range that you can grow. Alternatively, you can view them as useful plants with a purpose to use in particular situations.

A large proportion of alpines inhabit limestone rocks naturally. Most of them will do equally well on less alkaline soils so the alkalinity is not a prerequisite to growing good alpines, but at least you can be confident that with the inevitable exceptions they should do well.

Alpines don't need a rich soil, and they are extremely tolerant provided the drainage is good: even in a small rock garden you can find alpine plants native to a geographical area of hundreds of square miles, with many different soils. It's usually poor drainage that finishes off many of the less robust kinds, but chalk and limestone soils are usually well-drained anyway.

Fig 11. Trough gardens are fun to make and can make a feature in any garden. In this illustration, our plants include dianthus, *Phlox douglasii,* saxifrages, *Pulsatilla vulgaris,* campanulas, and *Armeria maritima,* all of which will grow in alkaline soils, but you could use an ericaceous mixture in the trough and grow acid-lovers such as some of the gentians.

ROCK GARDENS

The slopes of many chalk and limestone gardens provide an ideal setting for a really natural-looking rock garden. In some limestone areas there are rock outcrops to provide a ready-made base on which to build.

It's always a good idea to use a rock type that is found in your own part of the country, whatever type of soil you have. The advice is even more relevant in areas where natural rock outcrops occur, a common feature of many limestone regions. Here, a sandstone could look completely out of place.

Chalk itself is usually too soft to use, but the harder limestones are ideal. Weather-worn limestone is one of the most sought-after rocks for this purpose. Newly quarried limestone may be rather bright, but it mellows with time, and it looks as 'right' in a chalk area as in a limestone landscape.

CONSTRUCTION AND PLANTING

There's more to making a rock garden than setting a few rocks into a slope. The final result should look as though the outcrops are natural (all strata lines at the same angle), and it may be necessary to have as much of the rock beneath the surface as above it. At all costs avoid the common mistake of constructing a mound of soil with a few rocks stuck in the top. Rock that you have to buy in isn't cheap, so it's extremely well worthwhile buying a book on rock garden construction if you have any doubts.

Alpines in general are able to cling tenaciously to life once they are established, with their roots penetrating deep into crevices. It doesn't follow that they will tolerate neglect while becoming established. It's worth making a planting mixture of three parts garden soil, two parts peat or leafmould, and one-and-a-half parts of sand or grit. Use moss peat in preference to sedge peat, and sharp sand not soft builders' sand. If you have enough to use for bedding the rocks, so much the better, but if used just for the planting holes the alpines will have that good start in life that will make all the difference to achieving quick establishment.

This planting mixture is suitable for the vast majority of plants, but there are a few popular alpines that are best left out unless you are prepared to provide special peat beds.

ALPINES AROUND THE GARDEN

You don't need a rock garden in order to grow alpines. Raised beds, and containers such as elevated troughs, are ideal for alpines. They bring viewing that much closer, and it's possible to appreciate beauty that is often missed at ground level. You can, of course, grow almost any alpines this way because you can use soil to suit, but be sure to include a few miniature shrubs or very dwarf conifers to give height whenever the scale allows: flat raised beds can look extremely boring.

Sun roses (helianthemums) are great plants for a sunny position, and are as successful in a rock garden as covering a dry, sunny bank. This variety is 'Beechpark Red'.

Fig 12. If you have a sloping site, and don't want a large rock garden, try constructing an island rock bed. These can look very natural (even on a level site), and don't require much rock in comparison with a normal rock garden.

Within the chalk or limestone garden there will usually be plenty of opportunities for using alpines creatively. Some, such as ajugas, make excellent groundcovers, others (lots of dianthus and thymes for instance) can be used as crevice plants to grow between paving, or along the edge where the plants can tumble over and soften the hard outline. Some of the many suitable plants are suggested on the following pages, but it is worth experimenting with others if you have some spare plants.

PLANTS TO GROW

There are thousands of alpine plants that will grow successfully in rock gardens on alkaline soils, but the list that follows includes mainly merit-worthy plants that actually prefer these conditions. It's worth starting your shortlist of dependable plants with these, then adding to the collection as the urge to experiment makes its own demands.

FREE-GROWING ROCK PLANTS

It will seem heresy to some alpine purists to start with a group of plants that are so free-growing (a euphemism for rampant in some cases) and free-flowering that they are too unsociable to be grown among the more restrained and perhaps choicer plants. But some of the plants suggested are ideal for walls, banks that you want to cover quickly, and possibly as edging for beds; they are well worth considering for a newly established garden – even if you replace them with more refined plants later.

Alyssum saxatile, sometimes called gold dust, because of its mass of golden-yellow flowers, is cheap to buy, easy to raise and quick to flower from seed, and particularly adaptable. Pop a few seeds into a crevice in a wall, then wait for it to cascade down like a yellow waterfall; or let it spread in bold drifts like a river of yellow on a large rock garden. Young plants can even be used in spring bedding schemes with bulbs. Try it at the edge of a wide path, where it can tumble over the paving. There are several good varieties (try 'Citrinum' if you prefer a pale yellow), but all will thrive on lime and good drainage.

Aubrieta will thrive wherever the alyssum thrives, and they make good companions, the yellow of the alyssum contrasting with the blues, mauves and purples of the aubrieta.

Another easy rock plant to raise from seed, but be ruthless about discarding any with wishy-washy colours. Try pressing a few seeds into crevices in a wall: within a season or two you should have a curtain of colour.

Trim aubrieta with shears after flowering, to keep the plants compact.

Campanulas, with their blue bell flowers, thrive on alkaline soils. There are many of them, some choice gems that are tiny and dainty, others so vigorous they will cover the ground and then try to grow up a wall with almost a climbing habit. *C. poscharskyana* is inclined to be weedy, but *C. portenschlagiana* is bold yet well-behaved with rather clumpy growth. Both will establish themselves in walls, steps, and paving.

Cerastium tomentosum, sometimes called snow in summer because of its snow-white flowers in early summer over silvery-grey foliage. Again it's easy to grow from seed and will be flowering well in the second season. It's sometimes used as a ground-cover, but as it tends to become straggly and sometimes dies back in the centre or around the edges this is not its best use. But try it for quick cover on a bank.

Gypsophila repens is useful for walls where it can hang down, or for a large planting pocket that allows it to scramble over a large rock. It's also suitable for the top of a wall, and can be used to clothe a bank (though as it dies back to an overwintering rootstock in autumn, there are better plants for this job). The small white or pinkish flowers are not spectacular, but there are masses of them.

Iberis sempervirens *(Perennial candytuft)* is a clumpy dwarf evergreen shrub with heads of white flowers in late spring and early summer. Worth growing in all but the smallest rock garden, and one of the best evergreens for planting on or in a wall. 'Little Gem' makes a slow-growing shrub reaching to only about 15 cm (6 in) high.

Saponaria ocymoides *(Rock soapwort)* is a bushy trailer that will clothe a bank or cascade over a wall quickly. The star-like pink flowers appear in late spring and early summer. They are particularly vibrant and this makes a good contrasting companion for the cerastium mentioned above. It may tend to die back after a season or two, but it is extremely easy to raise more plants from seed.

The pasque flower. Pulsatilla vulgaris, also known as Anemone pulsatilla. It is one of the delights of the rock garden in spring.

PICK OF THE BUNCH

There are literally hundreds of excellent rock plants that you can grow on alkaline soils. To narrow the field, start your collection from among the short-list that follows. It will make the choice less confusing, and there are plenty of good plants to add later.

Armeria maritima, the popular thrift, is always well-behaved. Its evergreen hummocks spread slowly (I have even seen it used as a very pretty groundcover). The pink, red, or white flower heads cover the grass-like leaves in late spring and early summer. There are named varieties, but any of the thrifts should satisfy.

Campanulas always have a place in any rock garden, and they do well on chalk. Some of the vigorous species have already been mentioned, but among the stunning and more restrained species are *C. carpatica* and *C. garganica* ('W. H. Paine' is an outstanding lavender-blue form). One of my favourites when it's nestling among rocks is the dainty *C. cochlearifolia*. There are many others with which you can experiment.

Dianthus are typical of the natural limestone flora of many countries, and they are among the most indispensable alpines. There are lots to collect, but as a start, include *D. alpinus, D. deltoides* in its various forms, and *D. caesius* (which also goes under the unattractive name of *D. gratianopolitanus*). *D. neglectus* is one of the few said not to like lime, though some gardeners manage to grow it in chalky soils with little problem.

Gentiana acaulis, one of the spring gentians, thrives on many chalk soils, and its mass of blue upward-facing trumpets are a glorious sight on a large clump (though it can be reluctant to flower if things are not just to its liking). Many other spring-flowering gentians are also likely to be successful, but the autumn-flowering kinds such as *G. sino-ornata* are not for alkaline soils.

Helianthemum nummularium hybrids, known as sun roses or rock roses, are absolutely stunning when they're flowering in full sun (and they need full sun, otherwise the flowers will close). They are small evergreen shrubs (with some the foliage is grey rather than green). I include it here with hesitation. It also makes an appearance in the chapter on shrubs; and the spread of some of the varieties makes them unsuitable for planting among the less vigorous

alpines. But it's such a good plant for a large, sunny rockery, that its inclusion couldn't be resisted. There are many varieties, in shades of red, pink, yellow, and orange. Although there are doubles, the single forms are usually the most eye-catching from a distance. Dead-head after flowering – you may get another flush of flowers later.

Oenothera missouriensis, one of the evening primroses, is a personal favourite. There are other good dwarf oenotheras to try too (some of them a better choice if you don't have space for the spreading *O. missouriensis*). It has large lemon flowers, reddish in bud, over a long period throughout the summer. Its prostrate habit makes it useful for clothing a bank, provided you don't mind a sparse appearance during the winter.

Phlox douglasii is a versatile carpeter for spring flowering. There are varieties that range from white to lilac, blue, and pink. Varieties of *Phlox subulata* are similar. They will all bring a splash of colour to the rock garden, can be used as wall plants, and can make bright paving plants.

Polygonum vacciniifolium is a plant that you may have to trim back to keep it contained, but it's easily controlled and very useful for hot, well-drained soils. The small pink poker-like flower spikes bloom over a long period from early autumn. It is not over-enthusiastic about a limy soil, however, and the more vigorous and spreading *P. affine* is a better choice where you have the space – try it in a gravel garden, or along the edge of a path, even as a groundcover. 'Donald Lowndes' is a particularly good form.

Pulsatilla vulgaris, in its cultivated forms, will delight almost anyone in mid and late spring. The pasque flower has pretty anemone-type purple, white, lavender, maroon, or red flowers over unfurling feathery foliage. As well as being suitable for rock gardens pulsatillas can also be used in sink gardens and at the front of mixed or herbaceous borders.

Saxifrages are some of the 'essentials' of a rock garden, and many will do well on lime. You will need to consult a specialist catalogue for the many different species and varieties that are suitable, but start by looking at the 'encrusted' or Aizoon group. The cushion-forming Kabschias are best given a miss to start with, as they tend to have more demanding requirements. Some flower very early in the year – in late winter.

Fig. 13. There are plenty of plants that can be grown among paving, although some are more tolerant of trampling than others. It is best to plant them towards the edge of the path so that they are unlikely to be walked on. Suitable plants include those illustrated here: *Ajuga reptans, Armeria maritima, Campanula carpatica, Dianthus deltoides* and *Phlox douglasii.*

PLANTS FOR PAVING

- Ajuga reptans (Bugle)
- Alyssum montanum
- Alyssum saxatile 'Compactum'
- Anthemis nobilis 'Treneague' (Chamomile)
- Arenaria balearica
- Armeria caespitosa
- Armeria maritima (Thrift)
- Aubrieta
- Campanula carpatica
- Campanula portenschlagiana
- Dianthus deltoides (Maiden pink)
- Erinus alpinus
- Iberis sempervirens 'Little Gem' (Perennial candytuft)
- Phlox douglasii
- Phlox subulata
- Sedum (many – but avoid the very invasive S. acre)
- Thymus serpyllum (syn. T. drucei) (Thyme)
- Veronica prostrata

ALPINES FOR GROUND COVER

- Ajuga reptans (Bugle)
- Anthemis nobilis 'Treneague' (Chamomile)
- Aubrieta
- Dryas octopetala
- Helianthemum nummularium hybrids (Rock rose, Sun rose)
- Polygonum affine
- Polygonum vacciniifolium

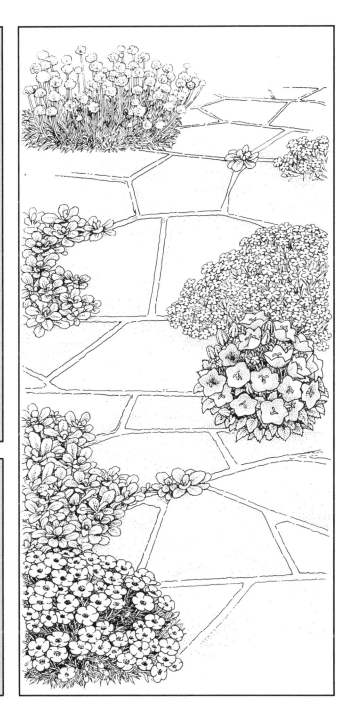

BORDER PLANTS AND BULBS

Few of us have the space or time to create the large herbaceous borders of the past, but the plants that were grown in them are as worthwhile today as ever they were. And without the herbaceous perennials and the bulbs to bring passing seasonal colour, the backbone shrubs and trees will lack contrast and the garden will lack vitality. Some are useful for groundcover, others for foliage effect, and of course many are grown simply because their flowers are striking or beautiful. For anyone constructing a new garden there's also the merit of quick growth. Even the slow ones grow rapidly in comparison with shrubs.

There's much to be said for mixed borders of shrubs and herbaceous plants (and perhaps annuals too). If herbaceous plants are to be grown on their own, island beds with tall plants in the centre are generally more useful than long, single-faced borders. Rather than have a border along a fence, it would be better to use the fence for climbers, and move the border into

Right: Thymus serpyllum, *a useful carpeter as a ground cover or for the rock garden. It often grows wild on chalk downland.*
Opposite: *A bright way to clothe a bank. Aubrietas are versatile plants, but sometimes a little too vigorous for a small rock garden.*

the garden, with access from either side.

Many herbaceous plants require a fairly rich soil and plenty of moisture to do well, so it's worth preparing the ground well. Again, it's difficult to add too much garden compost, manure, or other organic material. It's worth sprinkling a general fertilizer such as Growmore over any herbaceous or mixed beds in spring, as the new growth starts. Mulching helps too, especially for plants likely to be stressed by a shortage of water on dry soils.

Generally, however, most of the plants mentioned in the following pages will tolerate dry and impoverished conditions (though probably do that much better with a little encouragement). Don't be afraid to try others. Herbaceous border plants do not generally have such an extensive root system as trees and shrubs, so they are unlikely to penetrate to the underlying rock of very alkaline ground, and most will grow on alkaline soils of reasonable depth (say at least 30 cm/1 ft). Problems are most likely on dry, shallow chalk soils.

Although most plants loosely described as 'herbaceous plants' die down in winter, a few included here do not. The widely planted elephant ears (bergenias) are evergreen. The criterion for inclusion here is that they are not woody plants. If they happen to be evergreen, even better.

ACHILLEA
Yarrow; milfoil

The yarrows or milfoils do well on alkaline soils, and they can cope with dry, shallow soil if necessary. Some of the best border achilleas are 'Moonshine' (silvery foliage and pale-yellow flowerheads), 'Gold Plate' (golden yellow), and A. millefolium 'Cerise Queen' (cherry red). If you want a galaxy of colour, try the new 'Galaxy Hybrids' (individual varieties are available in pink, yellow and red). All flower between early and late summer.

The problem with achilleas is that they tend to blow over in strong winds, so some kind of staking is always worthwhile. 'Gold Plate' can be a particular problem because it grows to 1.2 m (4 ft) and more.

ACONITUM
Monkshood

The monkshoods have tall spikes of blue flowers, mostly

flowering in mid and late summer. There are several worthwhile species and varieties, but as a start try *A. napellus* 'Bressingham Spire' (about 1 m/3 ft).

There are drawbacks. They do not usually do well on shallow chalk soils, and wherever you grow them it's best to mulch each spring. The plants are poisonous.

AGAPANTHUS
African lily

The African lily is not hardy outdoors in cold areas, but in mild districts the hardier kinds can be left out safely. 'Headbourne Hybrids' are among the toughest. The flowers of these, and most others, are violet-blue to pale blue. *A. campanulatus* is almost hardy; pale blue is the usual colour, but 'Isis' is deep blue, and 'Albus' white.

These are among my favourite plants. They make a really bold show with their ball-shaped flowerheads above strap-like foliage from mid-summer to early autumn. They look superb in tubs, but are also very effective (in suitably mild areas) in big clumps or drifts in front of shrubs.

ALSTROEMERIA
Peruvian lily

These types of plants can be difficult to establish, but once happy and settled they are bright and beautiful. A warm, sunny position and good drainage are all essential. The lily-shaped flowers in clusters on leafy stems come in shades of cream, yellow, pink, salmon, scarlet, and orange.

In cold areas the Peruvian lilies may need winter protection (a thick mulch may be enough).

Although other species and varieties are available, it's best to start with the dependable 'Ligtu Hybrids'.

ANCHUSA

'Loddon Royalist', a variety of *A. italica,* is the one to grow for real impact. It has deep blue big forget-me-not flowers on stems 1 m (3 ft) or more high in early summer. It's such an intense blue that it commands attention.

Sadly, it tends to be short-lived, so it's worth propagating a few plants routinely.

ANEMONE

The anemones that you buy from bulb catalogues, such as *A. blanda* and *A. fulgens* will do very well on chalk soils, but for a really impressive late display try the border or Japanese anemones. There is a bit of confusion over nomenclature, and depending on the supplier you may find them described as *A. japonica, A. hupehensis,* or as *A. x hybrida.*

They are especially valuable because they flower later than most herbaceous border plants: late summer and into mid-autumn. And they will grow in sun or shade.

There are double and single forms, in shades of red, pink, and white, and the flowers are carried well clear of the foliage, on stems about 45-90 cm (1½-3 ft), depending on variety. Choose one that you like; a personal favourite is 'September Charm', a soft pink with a golden centre.

ANTHEMIS

Some anthemis are grown for their foliage effect: chamomile (A. nobilis) is one; others have attractive flowers. If you want to grow chamomile as a 'lawn' or for foliage effect 'Treneague' is the variety to choose (if you have ever tried growing a chamomile lawn, you'll know that there is a lot to be said for keeping to grass). The hybrid 'Grallagh Gold' is a popular variety grown for its yellow daisy-type flowers. But for me, there is one outstanding plant that outstrips all others: A. cupaniana. This plant has simple white daisy flowers over finely divided greyish leaves, but it blooms prolifically all summer.

'Grallagh Gold' will grow to 60 cm (2 ft) or a little more, A. cupaniana is only about half this height. Use them both towards the front of the border. A. cupaniana is also ideal in a semi-wild garden, to provide pockets of long-lasting summer colour in a large rock garden, or in bold drifts in front of dark-coloured shrubs in a sunny spot.

AQUILEGIA
Columbine

Aquilegias or columbines are cottage garden plants that need to be seen in a bold group rather than as individual plants. The spurred flowers, held well above the foliage, come in many shades, including yellow, pink, red, and blue. Go for one of the mixed hybrid strains for the herbaceous border. 'McKana Hybrids' is one of the most popular mixtures, but there are others.

ARTEMISIA

Good plants for foliage effect. 'Powis Castle' forms a rounded mass of silver filigree foliage. A. absinthium 'Lambrook Silver' has boldly cut silver leaves, with clusters of yellow flowers in mid and late summer (though its prime merit is as a foliage plant). Use both to break up areas of green foliage in the border, and to provide a longer period of interest among plants with a short flowering period and uninspiring foliage. They are ideal candidates for white and silver borders, or for mixing with pink flowers.

Because both plants tend to be woody, you might find either of them listed under shrubs or herbaceous plants, depending on the catalogue.

ASTER
Michaelmas daisy

The Michaelmas daisies will do well on alkaline soils. They are likely to be found in catalogues listed under *A. novae-angliae* or *A. novi-belgii.* Don't be put off by the idea that they are all tall plants with wishy-washy blue flowers and leaves covered in mildew. Although mildew can be a problem, the named varieties of these plants are first-rate, and will be smothered with blue, pink, red, or white flowers in early and mid-autumn when most other border plants have finished. There are dwarfs of about 30 cm (1 ft) as well as tall varieties of 1.2 m (4 ft).

This is a rich group of plants, and there are many other late-flowering species worth a try. Some to look out for are the *A. amellus* varieties, such as 'King George' (blue, 60 cm/2 ft), and *A. x frikartii* (pale lavender blue, 60-90 cm/2-3 ft, and unlikely to be troubled by mildew).

BERGENIA
Elephant ears

The large rounded evergreen leaves give the bergenias the common name of elephant ears. I think they are one of the most useful plants, providing year-round groundcover and a good show of flowers in spring. They will grow in sun or shade, and tolerate most soils. It's important to choose a good variety – 'Ballawley' is one of the best for overall impact.

CAMPANULA

Many campanulas thrive on alkaline soils. For the border, *C. lactiflora,* with its blue bells and the pink 'Loddon Anna' are good tallish plants for the middle of the border. *C. glomerata* 'Superba' is a good low, front-of-border plant with clusters of violet flowers.

CENTAUREA

Some of the centaureas tend to lack flowering impact to my mind, but I would not hesitate to find room for *C. montana,* which has blue ray-like flowers in late spring and early summer. It makes a nice clump about 45 cm (18 in) high.

CHRYSANTHEMUM

The summer-flowering shasta daisy *(C. maximum)* is often regarded as a coarse plant, perhaps because it is large and so easy to grow. The big white daisy flowers with yellow centres are, however, eyecatching. Try 'Snowcap', which has a compact habit and is usually less than 60 cm (2 ft). For a tall double, 'Wirral Supreme' is perhaps the most reliable.

Because I like to extend the flowering period in the border for as long as possible I have a particular fondness for the late-flowering border chrysanthemums. There are many kinds, but the hardy *C. rubellum* is particularly easy and worthwhile. 'Duchess of Edinburgh' has coppery-red flowers, 'Mary Stoker' is creamy-yellow. Study the catalogues for others.

Korean chrysanthemums are dwarf and spectacular massed together, but need more care otherwise they will be lost during the winter.

CIMICIFUGA
Bugbane
The bugbanes are useful where you want spiky plants to bring a bit of height and change of form. *C. cordifolia* and *C. racemosa* both have slender spikes of white flowers, and grow to about 1.2 m (4 ft).

DELPHINIUM
The tall border delphiniums need little introduction, and they will grow well on alkaline conditions provided there is a good depth of soil. They are perhaps best avoided on shallow chalk and dry soils.

For a small garden, the Belladonna hybrids are a better choice for general border decoration, growing to about 1.2 m (4 ft). Delphiniums can be raised quite easily from seed sown in spring in a cool greenhouse. Or from cuttings.

DIANTHUS
Carnations and pinks thrive on alkaline soils. The border carnations are much less popular than they used to be, but don't let that deter you from trying them. Among the pinks, the popular 'Doris' still takes some beating. It will produce its fragrant pink flowers on and off all summer. But take cuttings to replace the old plants as they become too woody.

DICTAMNUS
Burning bush
The burning bush (not to be confused with the annual kochia, which has the same common name) does well on limy soils. *D. fraxinella* really will 'burn' if you put a match near its leaves on a warm still day (it produces volatile oils). It's a leafy plant with pretty rose-purple flowers (there is also a white form).

An interesting plant worth growing in the border, or even as an unusual 'dot' plant for summer bedding.

DORONICUM
Leopard's bane
The leopard's banes are above all cheerful plants, producing yellow daisy-type flowers in mid and late spring. 'Miss Mason' is one of the best, and makes a plant of about 45 cm (18 in).

I like to see a carpet of doronicums, perhaps at the foot of a wall, or in a bold drift in front of shrubs. They are also useful for the edge of a border.

ECHINOPS
Globe thistle

Plants with a distinctive shape or profile are always worth trying to include in the garden. They serve as punctuation points. The globe thistles are useful in this way, with their globe-shaped 'thistle' flowers on rather spiky-looking plants.

Especially worth looking for are *E. humilis* 'Taplow Blue' and *E. ritro*. They grow to about 1-1.2 m (3-4 ft) tall, and flower in mid and late summer.

ERIGERON

If you like the dwarf Michaelmas daisies, you will almost certainly like the erigerons. From a distance they look like the compact varieties of Michaelmas daisies, but they flower during the summer.

There are several good named varieties available, in various shades of pink or blue. They are useful front-of-border plants.

ERYNGIUM
Sea holly

The sea hollies are distinctive plants with unusual teasel-like flowers, a 'thimble' centre being surrounded by a collar of usually silvery bracts. The spiny leaves are also very attractive.

Two to try to start with are *E. bourgatii* and the evergreen *E. variifolium*.

EUPHORBIA
Spurge

This is a large group of plants, and you will probably be able to grow only a few, so choose carefully. I have four favourites:

E. wulfenii has blue-green evergreen leaves and stiff spikes of pale-yellow flowers about 1.2 m (4 ft) high in spring.

E. griffithii 'Fireglow' makes a spreading plant of about 60-90 cm (2-3 ft) with flat heads of small orange-red flowers in early summer. A truly brilliant perennial.

E. polychroma (you might find it sold under its other name of *E. epithymoides*) is a real charmer when its sulphur-yellow flowers form a compact mound about 45 cm (18 in) high in spring.

E. myrsinites is a sprawling, ground-hugging plant, with the look of a succulent. Its blue-grey leaves are always attractive, but the plant is really eyecatching in early and mid-spring when the sulphur-yellow flower bracts command attention. It makes a good plant for a large rock garden, and it is great for a gravel garden, but be bold and try letting it cascade over the front of a border (provided you have a paving edge and don't have to mow up to the bed).

GAILLARDIA
Blanket flower

Gaillardias are not neat

plants, and you will probably have to give them some twiggy support, but the individual flowers are always bright and cheerful. And, of course, the blooms are excellent for cutting. There are several named varieties with large daisy-type flowers, in shades of orange, red, and yellow. Most grow to a little over 60 cm (2 ft).

GERANIUM
The hardy geraniums are easy and reliable plants, and some are useful as summer groundcover. 'Johnson's Blue' is a fine hybrid with bright-blue saucer-shaped flowers covering the plants in mid-summer. For groundcover, try *G. endressii,* which has pink flowers over pale green foliage. 'Wargrave Pink' is a form of it with salmon-pink flowers. Both grow to about 38 cm (15 in).

There are plenty of other geraniums to try if you have the space.

GYPSOPHILA
The gypsophilas are known as chalk plants, which shows how suitable they are for alkaline soils.

G. paniculata makes a bushy plant of about 1 m (3 ft) with feathery sprays of white flowers. 'Bristol Fairy' is a double form that's one of the best for the border.

HELENIUM
You can't miss heleniums when they are in flower. They are covered with masses of yellow, orange, or red, rayed flowers with raised centres. They flower between mid-summer and early autumn, depending on the variety. Although some grow as low as 60 cm (2 ft) others are over 1 m (3 ft) and need support in an exposed position.

Very useful plants for bringing bold splashes of colour to the herbaceous border.

HELIANTHUS
Perennial sunflower
The perennial sunflowers are serious contenders for the border, and not just fun flowers in the way that the annual sunflowers are usually regarded. It is the varieties of *H. decapetalus* that are usually grown (you may find some listed under *H. multiflorus*). 'Loddon Gold' is a good one, with big double flowers on plants about 1.5 m (5 ft) tall. 'Soleil d'Or' is a nice semi-double.

You will need to support the plants, and double varieties are best divided after a few years to reduce the chance of them reverting to singles.

HELLEBORUS
Most people associate the hellebores with the Christmas rose *(H. niger),* or the lenten rose *(H. orientalis),* but there are other very worthwhile

Anthemis cupaniana *is a plant to grow if you want a profusion of flowers over a long period. It will put on an impressive show for the whole summer.*

species too.

The white or purplish flowers of the Christmas and lenten roses (flowering in winter and spring respectively) are always a welcome sight poking out of the low spread of foliage. But try *H. corsicus* (syn. *H. argutifolius*) with its cup-shaped yellow-green flowers above attractive claw-like evergreen foliage; or *H. foetidus*, with its thimble-sized pale green flowers, sometimes rimmed purple, in spring, over dark evergreen leaves. A useful shade plant.

HEMEROCALLIS
Day lilies

The hemerocallis or day lilies are now deservedly popular plants. The big trumpet-shaped flowers in shades of yellow, pink, red, and orange, often last only a day before dying, but there is a constant succession of them. You can depend on the plants being a mass of flower for weeks in summer.

There are many excellent varieties, and it is worth studying specialist catalogues if you feel you want to start a collection.

Although individual plants can be attractive, day lilies have much more impact planted as a bold drift. If you have a large garden and can afford the space, try a small border of nothing but day lilies – it will be stunning when they are in flower.

HEUCHERA
Coral flower

The varieties of *Heuchera sanguinea*, being evergreen, have a year-round appeal as edging plants or as ground-cover, the foliage remaining low and compact. But it is in summer, when the spikes of pink or red flowers form a haze of colour above the foliage, that they are really splendid. For this effect they do need to be massed.

HOSTA
Plantain lily

Hostas (plantain lilies) have become some of our most popular foliage plants. They will tolerate an alkaline soil, but they don't like it too dry, which means that shallow chalk soils may be a problem.

Choose from the many species and varieties, lots of them attractively variegated.

IRIS

The bearded irises are really impressive for one month of the year (early summer), but boring for the rest. Some experts recommend growing them in a bed of their own, but I find them better planted among different herbaceous plants that will continue the period of interest. They are, however, very effective planted in drifts in front of shrubs, provided the site is sunny enough.

There are too many types and varieties of irises suitable

for beds and borders to mention here. Your local garden centre should have a good selection; but for a range of species and to search out many of the best hybrids it will be necessary to consult a specialist catalogue.

KNIPHOFIA
Red-hot pokers
I confess that I have a special affection for the red hot pokers. A really impressive clump, perhaps viewed from a low angle against a blue sky, has the same kind of effect on me as a good piece of music. By choosing suitable species and varieties, you can enjoy kniphofias from early summer well into the autumn. Try them as ordinary border subjects, grow them in front of shrubs, or use the large ones as isolated clumps.

For early flowering (early and mid-summer), good ones are 'Bee's Sunset' (flame-orange), and 'Springtime' (yellow, topped red). For mid-season (mid-summer to early autumn) try 'Maid of Orleans' (creamy-white), 'Samuel's Sensation' (scarlet-red), or *K. uvaria*. For late flowering (early and mid-autumn), 'C. M. Pritchard' (bronzy-orange), and for a dwarf *K. galpinii* are worth considering. There are many others, and the seasons above may overlap.

In cold areas, kniphofias may need winter protection for the crown.

LINUM
Blue flax
L. narbonense, the blue flax, will flower for weeks in summer. It is not a robust-looking plant, but growing to about 45 cm (18 in) it can usually be worked in towards the front of a border where the bright blue can be appreciated.

LOBELIA
The edging and basket bedding lobelia can be grown at the front of a border, but it is really the tall spiky *L. cardinalis* (and the similar *L. fulgens,* with which it is often confused) that make striking plants if grown in a bold clump. The dark reddish foliage is another attraction. They also make superb 'dot' plants for summer bedding, especially in association with grey-leaved plants.

In cold areas they will certainly have to be lifted and given frame or greenhouse protection, but in some years you will get away with leaving them outdoors during the winter in mild districts. Just don't depend on it.

LYCHNIS
The smaller species, such as *L. flos-jovis* (crimson-magenta, mid-summer to early autumn) and *L. x arkwrightii* (orange-scarlet, early to late summer) are suitable for a large rock garden or at the front of a border. There are also some for the centre of

the herbaceous border, particularly *L. coronaria* (crimson-magenta flowers from mid to late summer, over woolly silver-grey leaves), a striking plant in full flower.

MONARDA
Sweet bergamot; bee balm
The sweet bergamot or bee balm, *M. didyma,* and its hybrids, are useful for bringing variety to the border, but are not particularly beautiful.

The rather 'tufty' flowers are pink, red, violet-purple, lavender, or white, depending on variety, all at the top of leafy stems.

NEPETA
Catmint
Liked by me as much as by cats, the catmints are really first-rate plants for the front of a border, especially where they can tumble right over the edge.

The mound of grey aromatic foliage is attractive the summer long, and the plants a haze of blue flowers for most of the season.

There is much confusion between *N. x faassenii* and *M. mussinii,* one sometimes being grown as the other. It doesn't really matter because both are worthwhile plants. But look for 'Six Hills Giant', taller and deeper blue.

OENOTHERA
Evening primrose
There are tall oenotheras or evening primroses, and dwarf ground-huggers. 'Highlight' grows to about 60 cm (2 ft), so is not too tall for growing towards the front of the border, and it has masses of yellow saucer-shaped flowers. But my personal favourite is the prostrate *O. missouriensis,* with its large canary yellow flowers produced over a long period in summer. Super for a sunny bank.

PAEONIA
Peony
The border peonies never fail to impress. They are big, bold and rather exotic-looking. Such beauty does not come easily – they can take a few years to settle down and become established enough to flower well, and you will need to feed them.

It's worth consulting the catalogues for the many varieties of peony, there are dozens of them, but one species worth growing is *P. mlokosewitschii* – an awful name but a lovely plant, with lemon yellow goblet flowers.

PAPAVER
Poppy
The Oriental poppies *(P. orientalis)* are real stunners. You certainly can't ignore a large well-grown (and well-staked) clump with the huge open poppy flowers in shades of red, pink, orange, and white, in early summer. But they are large plants and in a

small garden you will probably question whether their brief spell of glory is worth the space they require.

PHLOX

The border phlox are magnificent if healthy and well grown. You can achieve good results on deep alkaline soils, but not on shallow or dry or impoverished ones. Given their susceptibility to eelworm and mildew, they are probably best given a miss unless you are particularly fond of them and can provide that extra bit of attention.

PLATYCODON

P. grandiflorum has curiously shaped, rather angular, inflated buds, which open into pale blue stars in late summer. The plants are quite compact at about 45 cm (18 in).

POLEMONIUM
Jacob's ladder

Although not spectacular plants, the polemoniums (Jacob's ladders) do well on chalky soils. The small open blue bells are held above clumps of divided foliage, starting in the late spring and continuing well into summer. *P. caeruleum* is perhaps the best to start with.

POLYGONUM

Some of the knotweeds can become invasive, but I would not hesitate to grow *P. affine*,

a useful carpeter with small pink poker flower spikes over a long period from mid-summer and into autumn.

'Darjeeling Red' and 'Donald Lowndes' are two good varieties, the latter being more compact, though both will form a spreading mat (useful for softening the edge of a path).

POTENTILLA

The herbaceous potentillas lack the qualities of a first-rate border plant, but they have the merit of a long flowering season in summer. There are both red and orange varieties. If you have to cut it down to one, try the red 'Gibson's Scarlet'.

PRIMULA

A wide range of primulas will do well, including polyanthus and primroses such as the very attractive purple 'Wanda'. Try using them at the front of the herbaceous border to bring early colour before the summer flowers begin to take over.

A word of caution: not all primulas will succeed well on alkaline soils.

PYRETHRUM

This entry could have gone under *Chrysanthemum*, for the pyrethrums are now counted as part of this genus. But in many catalogues you'll still find them listed as pyrethrums, which is the name that most gardeners still use.

These plants are not as popular as they used to be. Their only fault to my mind is the need for staking to make tidy plants. There are single and double varieties, mainly in shades of pink or red.

Try them if there is a reasonable depth of soil, but they won't like shallow chalk soils, and they dislike drought.

RUDBECKIA
Coneflower
Rudbeckias are another personal favourite. There are several good ones to choose from, including doubles, but I especially like *R. deamii* (a free-flowering plant with yellow ray petals and a dark central cone), and 'Goldsturm' (deep yellow with a dark central eye). They flower from mid-summer through to early autumn.

SALVIA
The border salvias are usually blue or purple, and much taller than the red bedding type. Varieties of *S. superba* are the ones to grow for impact. 'East Friesland' (violet-purple) and 'May Night' (violet-blue) are particularly good, making clumps of spiky flowers about 45 cm (18 in) tall in early and mid-summer.

SCABIOSA
Scabious
Scabious revel in lime. It is usually varieties of *S. caucasica* that are grown, and the old 'Clive Greaves' is still a good one. The blue flowers, popular for cutting, are produced from early to late summer.

SIDALCEA
The sidalceas are pretty in flower, with tall spikes of pink or reddish flowers above a compact cluster of low foliage. Yet they seem to lack the impact to make much of a contribution to the border unless planted in a group of reasonable size.

SOLIDAGO
Golden rod
The golden rod is still misunderstood by lots of gardeners. They dismiss it with memories of the old tall and weedy kinds that used to be seen. Modern varieties are compact, well-behaved, and very attractive.

Try some of the dwarfs (about 45 cm/18 in), such as 'Cloth of Gold' and 'Crown of Rays'. 'Tom Thumb' is only about 30 cm (1 ft) tall. All have sprays of yellow flowers in the late summer or early autumn.

THALICTRUM
The thalictrums really need a fairly deep soil and partial shade to do well. The ferny foliage is one of the main attractions, but the small purple, mauve, lavender, or white

flowers are not unattractive viewed as a mass.

T. dipterocarpum grows to about 1.8 m (6 ft), so needs plenty of space. *T. aquilegifolium* has aquilegia-like foliage and fluffy heads of purple to mauve flowers.

TRADESCANTIA
Spiderwort

The spiderworts are rather stiff-looking plants, and the flowers tend to be hidden among the foliage. Nevertheless they do very well on alkaline soils.

It is the varieties of *T. virginiana* that are grown. Blue, purple, and white are the main colours.

VERBASCUM

Although I have never found the mulleins to be especially noteworthy, they do thrive on chalk soils. They have spiky flowers, and my complaint is that usually only a few flowers are out at once, and there always seems to be more still to open or that have died, and they can look tatty. From a distance, however, you don't notice this so much, and they are useful where you want a spiky plant about 1-1.2 m (3-4 ft) tall. A nice species is *V. chaixii* with yellow flowers (there is a form with white flowers).

Among the hybrids, try 'Cotswold Queen' (shades of buff, purple and orange), and 'Gainsborough' (yellow).

VERONICA

The border veronicas are very pretty plants with a neat, compact habit. 'Crater Lake Blue' is a reliable and very satisfactory plant, with blue flower spikes between early and late summer.

You may find this listed as a variety of *V. spicata* or *V. teucrium*.

BULBS, CORMS, AND TUBERS

There are very few bulbs that won't grow well on alkaline soils, provided the drainage is good. The only problem is likely to come on alkaline clays, when it may be necessary to add sand or grit to improve drainage when planting. It is a good idea to use plenty of bulbs (the term is used loosely to include corms and tubers) among herbaceous border plants or in mixed borders, not only because they generally perform well, but also to extend the season of interest. The majority of bulbs that we buy flower in spring, when few herbaceous plants are putting in a performance. Summer-flowering bulbs, including lilies, can play their role with the other border plants, then the later flowers can again bring colour when the main border plants have passed their best: the autumn crocuses (colchicums), schizostylis, and nerines.

For spring, narcissi, including daffodils, are indispensable. They not only look good, they multiply readily and need very little attention. If you tire of too many yellow daffodils in spring, try the bicolours, or whites. Or plant some of the dwarfer species, or perhaps the pheasant's eye narcissus (*N. poeticus*). Tulips will almost certainly be successful, but the large-flowered hybrid types seldom flower well if just left in the ground. Some of the species, such as *T. tarda*, will. Choose these for the border and let them form large colonies.

Some of the anemones, such as *A. blanda*, actually need a season to become established properly anyway, but if left undisturbed will gradually spread over the years to form a carpet of

Right: *Aquilegias are insteresting as well as beautiful plants, with spurred flowers in delicate colour combinations. But grow several plants together for impact.*
Opposite:
Delphiniums are traditional border plants, and if supported well while young are ideal for bringing a bit of height to a border.

flowers. If you can take a long-term view, try to establish drifts of them among and beneath deciduous shrubs. Anemones, winter aconites (Eranthis hyemalis), and of course crocuses, can be established around the base of deciduous trees.

Follow on in the border in late spring with a few bold clumps of the crown imperial (Fritillaria imperialis), and then let alliums hold interest in early summer (there are many different kinds suitable for the border), followed by the many summer-flowering bulbs such as galtonias, gladioli, and even big bold plants like eremurus. The latter are really imposing plants with big, tall spikes in shades of orange, buff, pink, or white, often reaching 1.5 m (5 ft). But they need careful planting, placing the crown just below the surface and spreading the fragile roots out in a wide hole.

The colchicums are always worth growing for autumn interest, and the results are usually very instant. They will usually flower soon after planting in the autumn (the leaves don't appear until the spring). There are many good species and varieties, all impressive at the front of the border as long as they are planted reasonably close and left to form a big clump.

Schizostylis (Kaffir lilies) can be bought as growing plants from herbaceous plant suppliers, or from bulb merchants. They are invaluable late flowerers (mid and late autumn) for the border. They do, however, prefer a moist soil, so shallow chalk soils may need extra humus added, or plenty of water in dry weather. In cold areas the crowns will need the winter protection of bracken, straw, dry peat, or a similar mulch. There are several varieties, but one of the boldest and most reliable is S. coccinea 'Major', which has strong spikes of red flowers, to about 75 cm (2½ ft).

If you have a sunny spot, and especially if you garden in a mild area, do try to grow nerines. These have heads of rather spidery pink flowers that last for weeks between early and late autumn. N. bowdenii is the only species worth trying outdoors in most areas, and 'Fenwick's Variety' is a specially good form. Again they will need winter protection in many areas, but where the winters are not too severe they can be left undisturbed to make large, free-flowering groups.

Lilies are really too grand to be dismissed in a couple of paragraphs, but it is inevitable that within the limited space available in a general book one can do no more than whet the appetite.

Not all lilies will tolerate lime, so if one that you want to grow is not mentioned below, make a point of checking in a specialist book on lilies to see whether it is suitable.

The following list is a selection of species, but there are many hybrids that you may prefer if you want bigger and bolder flowers. It is best to consult a specialist lily catalogue or book to decide which hybrids to grow. Species to try include: *L. amabile, L. bulbiferum, L. hansonii, henry, L. martagon, L. monadelphum,* *L. pardalinum, L. regale, L. speciosum,* and *L. testaceum.*

If you have space for only one of these species, plant *L. regale.* It has almost everything that you could want from a lily. The fragrant white, trumpet-shaped flowers shade to yellow at the throat and are flushed pinkish-brown outside. They are big and beautiful, growing to about 1.2 m (4 ft). And easy to grow too.

There are numerous small bulbs suitable for the rock garden. Most will do well in alkaline soils anyway, but being shallow rooted it's easy to improve the soil locally to grow the vast majority of them without any difficulty.

ANNUALS AND BEDDING PLANTS

Both hardy annuals, sown where they are to flower, and tender bedding plants raised under glass and planted out, present no real problem. They are shallow rooted and quick to flower (many bedding plants bought from shops and garden centres may already be starting to flower in the seed trays).

Most spring bedding plants, such as polyanthus and double daisies, will tolerate a high pH (wallflowers prefer it), and the same applies to the summer bedding such as salvias and French marigolds. Even those that prefer a more acid soil will probably perform satisfactorily: they aren't in the ground long enough for performance to suffer; and most annuals under stress tend to bloom prolifically (even if they don't look very lush) in an effort to set as much seed as possible.

Be bold with the use of annuals. Even if formal bedding is not appropriate, they make good gap fillers in borders, and can often be integrated very successfully with perennials.

THE KITCHEN GARDEN

For some reason most of the books that have been written on gardening on chalk or limy soils tend to ignore fruit and vegetables – some don't bother to mention them. I don't understand why, because it seems unlikely that gardeners are any more or less interested in growing food crops just because their soil is alkaline.

Whatever your soil, there will be certain fruit and vegetables that just won't do well, but shallow, chalky soils are a special problem because their often inadequate depth and stony structure makes it difficult to grow a whole range of rootcrops satisfactorily. And crops such as French and runner beans, potatoes, and tomatoes all prefer a soil on the acid side of neutral. The same applies to such fruits as apples, pears, raspberries, and strawberries. It's best to concentrate on growing those fruit and vegetables that will actually do well on these difficult soils, but growing a food crop is not the same as growing flowers – you probably won't want to rule out such 'basics' as potatoes, beans, and tomatoes.

Fortunately, there are simple solutions to some of the problems.

Right: Doronicum plantagineum, *one of the leopard's banes, bright and cheerful flowers for late spring and early summer.*

Opposite: *The hellebores (this is a variety of H. orientalis) do well on alkaline soils, and can even be used as ground cover.*

MODIFYING THE RULES

Books on vegetable growing will tell you to practise a crop rotation based on a three-year or four-year cycle, with the position of the plants being moved each year, and nutrients, manures, and lime being applied according to the next crop to be grown. The principles of crop rotation are as important for limy soils as they are for any other (it ensures the best use of nutrients and helps to avoid the build-up of soil-borne pests and diseases). You will simply have to modify it.

It's easy to become confused by crop rotation plans: there are many variations. But what they usually have in common is a heavy application of manure or garden compost where potatoes or legumes (peas, beans) or crops such as tomatoes or celery are to be grown; a dressing of lime on the plot to be planted with brassicas (cabbages, cauliflowers, turnips); and an intermediate plot for rootcrops, such as carrots and parsnips, where neither manure nor lime has been applied recently. Such rotations are designed to leave as long as possible between liming and growing potatoes (the high pH encour-ages scab disease), at least a couple of years between applying manure and growing crops like carrots (freshly applied manure may cause roots to fork), and lime is applied just before the most lime-tolerant group (the brassicas) are grown.

It's a good idea to follow the basic rotation, but it will not be necessary to add lime (which may be positively detrimental), and manure or garden compost should be added to all plots except for the rootcrops such as carrots and parsnips. 'Roots' such as beetroot, won't come to any harm if planted on manured ground.

Green manuring does not feature in most basic crop rotation plans, but whenever you have an area of ground that is likely to be unoccupied for eight weeks or more between early spring and late autumn, it's worth using it for a green manure crop.

Widely available green manures are mustard and rape, but grazing ryegrass, clover, and annual lupins are among the alternatives if you are prepared to search around for a supplier. The clover, and winter tares (corn-weeds) and ryegrass are usually sown in late summer or early to mid-autumn; mustard and rape are suitable for sowing throughout the spring and summer (these are not a good choice if club root disease is a problem but this is uncommon on alkaline soils).

You can cut and compost the crop, but it's an extra task. Just dig the plants in before they have the chance to set seed, and let the leaves decompose in the soil.

A combination of plenty of added manure or garden compost, together with green manuring where it is practical, will raise the humus content of the soil, and to some small extent lower the pH. It will also aid water retention – a crucial factor for many crops if you are unable to irrigate regularly.

Double digging (digging to twice the depth of a spade's blade) is hard work that you can actually dispense with on many soils. Provided you avoid bringing any of the subsoil towards the surface, it will help to increase the depth of workable soil where this is inadequate. But don't expect results in a single season.

On some chalk soils you simply won't be able to double dig – at least not unless you resort to the pick-axe instead of the spade. Then it's worth asking yourself if it isn't

Fig 14. If you're having trouble growing vegetables on a shallow chalk soil, it may be possible to improve things by using shallow raised beds.

easier to buy your vegetables.

If you really do have an intransigent soil, and you don't want to give up your chance to grow fresh vegetables, it's time to find another way round the problem.

You can try a few raised beds – they don't need to be more than about 23 cm (9 in) high, but there's the expense of timber, bricks, or blocks to make the bed, and it probably means buying in topsoil from elsewhere to raise the ground level. If you make the beds no more than 1.2 m (4 ft) wide you can use the deep bed system (once the ground has been prepared you won't have to dig provided you mulch with plenty of organic material and do all your cultivating from the paths so that you don't compact the soil). (See box below.)

That's one of the best long-term solutions, but for more instant results there's a lot to be said for growing bags.

They are widely used for tomatoes, and fairly commonly for lettuces, but they

THE DEEP BED SYSTEM

The deep bed system of cultivation is intended to reduce or eliminate the need to dig, but it can also be very useful on chalky soils as a method of increasing the depth of fertile soil in which to grow vegetables.

The beds are usually 1.2 m (4 ft) wide for the practical reason that you need to be able to reach the crops from either side without treading on the soil, so causing compaction. And for the system to work properly, you must dig deeply initially – double dig (that is, to the depth of two-spade blades) to break up the soil and improve aeration and drainage. This is clearly difficult on some shallow chalk soils, but dig as deeply as possible, breaking up the lower level, and if necessary form slightly raised beds to increase the depth.

To maintain the fertility of the soil, you must dig in lots of organic matter, such as garden compost or manure, when you prepare the bed initially. And you have to apply thick mulches of compost, manure, or other organic material each season.

Provided you don't walk on the soil, and mulch frequently, worms and other insects will gradually work the organic matter into the soil, and you should not have to dig again for perhaps three or four years.

The constant addition of plenty of organic matter is, of course, especially beneficial on chalky soils.

are more versatile than that. New (that is, first-time use) growing bags can also be used for runner beans (you can buy special supports, but it's easier and probably cheaper to stand the bag on soil and push ordinary bamboo canes through the base of the bag). You should be able to get a second season out of most bags before you put the peat on the garden, and old bags are fine for many of the crops that would be damaged by a stony soil (radishes for instance). And if you choose suitable small stump-rooted or round varieties you can even grow carrots. I've grown beetroot, spinach, turnips,

WHICH DO WELL?

The following vegetables do well in a pH above 7 (though with few exceptions not above 7.5):

- Asparagus
- Beetroot
- Broccoli
- Cabbage
- Cauliflower [1]
- Carrot
- Celery [1]
- Leek
- Lettuce
- Onion
- Spinach beet
- Sweet corn

[1] *Avoid cauliflowers and celery unless you are prepared to water regularly*

The day lilies (hemerocallis) will flower prolifically for weeks (even though individual blooms are short-lived). This one is 'Red Admiral'.

and a variety of other vegetables in old growing bags (they don't have to be old, of course – it just makes more sense to use the new ones for gross feeders like tomatoes and runner beans, and use the more exhausted ones for less demanding crops such as lettuces and radishes).

Don't forget: growing bags must be fed, even for the first season. They are not intended to support a crop for the whole season without any supplementary feeding.

GROWING HERBS

Some herbs thrive on alkaline soils – thymes for instance. But with the exception of the large plants such as fennel and lovage, most herbs can be grown in containers of various kinds if necessary. And fennel will be no problem in a chalky garden.

It can be a positive advantage to grow mint in an old growing bag, otherwise it will be difficult to restrain to its allotted place.

A word of warning: planting in herb pots and window-boxes will create interesting features, but there will be a constant conflict between the demands of the kitchen and the desire to retain an attractive planting.

FRUIT

Shallow chalk soils are not ideal for growing fruit. Lime-induced chlorosis (shown by a yellowing of the leaves between the veins) may be a problem, and it may be necessary to apply iron and/or manganese to overcome deficiencies. Die-back may also be a problem. On shallow soils, drought is also likely to affect yield unless the plants are watered before they become stressed.

The key to growing any tree fruit (such as apples and pears) well on an alkaline soil is to prepare a deep planting hole, breaking up any hard subsoil thoroughly, add as

Fig 15. It's possible to grow a small and attractive collection of herbs in a pot like this. Chives have been planted in the centre, and the other herbs include parsley (French and ordinary), thymes, marjorams, and tarragon.

much peat, garden compost, or manure as you can spare, then mulch thickly every year with manure or garden compost. Keep down weed growth around the plant's base to avoid competition for water and nutrients.

The same general rules apply to soft fruit, though as many of them (such as raspberries and strawberries) have comparatively shallow roots the depth of soil is less important.

Strawberries can be grown very successfully in growing bags and other containers.

Apples are unlikely to do well, but you will improve results on a poor chalk soil by choosing a more vigorous rootstock than you would normally (on a poor soil the dwarfing effect may be too pronounced).

LIME-TOLERANT FRUIT

The following fruit will grow happily in a pH on the alkaline side of neutral, but generally they do not appreciate a pH above 7.5.

- Apricots (but only suitable for a warm, sunny spot in a favourable area)
- Cobnuts and filberts
- Blackcurrants
- Figs
- Plums (though they prefer pH 6-6.5)

IF YOU REALLY MUST GROW APPLES . . .

Apples are such a popular fruit that gardeners sometimes find it difficult to resist the temptation to try their luck, even on chalk or limestone soils. So if you really do want to try a couple of trees (and for pollination reasons, it's best to have more than one), here are a few tips to try.

☐ The eating apple 'Charles Ross', and the cooker 'Bramley Seedling' are said to be more tolerant of alkaline soils than most. They are both good varieties, so try these.

☐ Treat the trees with sequestered iron each spring.

☐ Make a real effort to improve the soil when planting, and if practicable think about replacing soil for the planting hole with imported topsoil.

☐ Consider growing your apple trees in large containers (large pots or tubs). Don't expect a fantastic crop, but it's a perfectly realistic option provided you are able to water the trees regularly in dry weather (a trickle irrigation system is the best solution). Use a good loam-based compost (don't just use garden soil), and insist on apples grafted onto the dwarfing M27 rootstock.

CARE AND CULTIVATION

With the right choice of plants, and good initial soil preparation, it's possible to garden for years without even being aware that you have a 'problem' soil. Certainly routine care like pruning and weeding are not different on alkaline soils. But even the best gardens need careful tending if they are to remain looking good, and plants on difficult alkaline soils will definitely deteriorate if they are on the borderline of tolerance.

There are three keys that will unlock the doors of success: feeding, mulching, and watering. Neglect any of them, and there will be plants that protest by showing signs of chlorosis or stress. This is especially so on shallow chalk soils, where dryness can be a problem as great as the alkalinity for some plants.

FEEDING

It has already been said that many alkaline soils,

Fig 16. pH affects the availability of nutrients. This chart shows how different pH levels influence the availability of most of the major and minor nutrients needed by plants. This chart is based on mineral soils – the availability of nutrients such as boron and manganese my be different on peaty soils.

Opposite:
Red-hot-pokers (kniphofias) are some of the boldest border plants, and they do well on alkaline soils. This one is 'Royal Standard'.

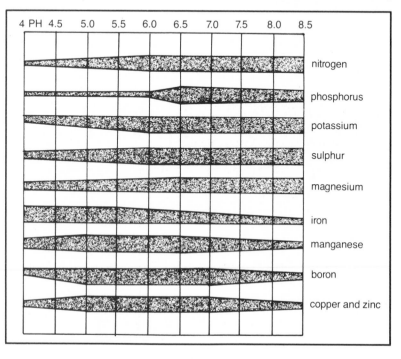

especially shallow soils on hillsides, are frequently impoverished. And adding manure or garden compost at planting time can have an all too transient effect, as it tends to decompose and become used up very quickly.

You can buy kits that will test for major nutrient deficiencies, and you may want to consider sending a soil sample away for professional analysis. The problem is that nutrient deficiencies can vary dramatically from one part of the garden to another, especially if you have applied different amounts of manures or fertilizers to different parts in the past (something that frequently happens on vegetable plots). And a soil nutrient analysis is not a once-and-for-all job: nutrient balances will vary not only from season to season, but from month to month. And the fertilizer that you apply will remain more effective on some soils than on others (partly because fertilizers containing elements such as nitrogen are quickly leached away by rainwater on some soils, and partly because the interaction with other chemicals in the soil may make them more or less available to plants).

Although it's a mistake to believe that if a little is good, a lot must be better, a general garden fertilizer applied routinely every year (in mid or late spring) is a good idea for 'hungry' soils. You can buy many different compound fertilizers, some intended for general use, others formulated for a specific crop, or for grass. By all means use these, but there's nothing wrong with using one general fertilizer such as Growmore for the whole garden (flower beds, vegetable plot, lawn). Lest anyone think this is an advertisement for a particular brand of fertilizer, it is the name of a *formula* that can be prepared by any company. It has an analysis of 7:7:7 (that is seven percent each of nitrogen, phosphorus, and potassium), and is usually applied at a rate of between 1 oz and 4 oz to a square yard. This is a popular fertilizer in Britain, but in other countries there are balanced fertilizers with similar ratios.

There may be an advantage in using a proprietary fertilizer if it also contains some of the minor nutrients (which may be described as trace elements) that may be deficient. If you are using a lot of fertilizers, it's likely to be cheaper to use just one than 'specials' for different crops or plants, simply because you can buy larger packs more cheaply.

For a lush lawn, or particularly fine roses, it may be worth paying a bit more for specific formulations, but the regular use of a general fertilizer such as Growmore will at least keep the fertility level reasonably high.

Adding fertilizers can sometimes have a short-lived effect. If the pH is very high, the calcium can react with phosphorus to form insoluble calcium phosphate, which becomes unavailable to many plants. They can, however, overcome the problem to some extent with the weak acids produced by the roots that release phosphate ions. Lime-loving plants are better at doing this. Also, many plants take up calcium from the soil in preference to elements such as iron (leading to iron deficiency in very alkaline soil). So no matter how much general fertilizer you add, lime-sensitive plants will still be unhappy unless they have special treatment.

The general soil improvements suggested in Chapter Two will do much to alleviate the problems, but the chances are there will still be individual plants or crops that still remain unhappy and unhealthy. On lawns and the vegetable plot, it's worth using acidic nitrogenous fertilizers over a long period, so reducing the overall pH (but don't overdo this, otherwise the levels of nitrogen will actually damage the plants and much of it will in any case be leached through the soil and into the natural drainage system before the plants can use it – good for neither plants nor environment. For more immediate results, foliar feeding and chelated trace elements are probably the best solution.

Many liquid feeds are suitable for foliar feeding (check the label). Although much of the fertilizer runs off into the soil, where hopefully much of it is taken up by the roots, some is absorbed through the leaves. This means that the nutrients are taken into the plant before they have had a chance to become chemically locked in the soil.

The effects of foliar feeding can be dramatic. The leaf colour may improve within days, and it's the best way to revive a plant that looks in need of urgent help. Applying fertilizer through a spray is clearly tedious and not to be recommended as routine for all the garden. But it's worth mixing a foliar feed two or three times during the growing season, and just going round the garden to spray those isolated plants that look in need of a boost.

LAWNS

Alkaline lawns generally have more worms in them than acid lawns (a drawback if you want a bowling-green type finish, because of the casts produced by some species), and there are likely to be more weeds (especially daisies, selfheal, dandelions, pearlwort, and plantains). The weeds may not bother you if the lawn is large and mainly for general recreation, but they can be a nuisance if you want quality turf. The increased activity of worms, and the proliferation of weeds, can sometimes be seen on old sports fields where the long application of the white lining material has made the soil locally more alkaline.

Clearly, if there is a choice, a slightly acid soil will generally produce the better lawn. But you should be able to produce perfectly satisfactory results on an alkaline soil. Grasses are generally shallow-rooting, and a few simple actions will generally be all that's needed:

☐ Use acidic fertilizers where possible. When the lawn needs nitrogen, use sulphate of ammonia (it will make the soil more acid, but apply only when the grass needs a boost of nitrogen).

☐ When topdressing, use plenty of peat, which is acid.

☐ If you want to increase the acidity quickly, try applying sulphur at 35g to a square metre (1 oz to a square yard) before you sow or plant.

☐ Start a new lawn from turf rather than seed. Although the very best quality turf comes with little soil, most turf is cut with a reasonable amount of earth and the grass will have this to grow in before it penetrates the more alkaline soil.

These simple steps are likely to be more effective than trying to select lime-tolerant grasses. Ryegrass is generally tolerant of a pH as high as 8, so mixtures containing ryegrass may be a better choice than those containing say browntop or common bent (*Agrostis tenuis*), which grows naturally on generally poor, acid soils. Crested dog's tail (*Cynosurus cristatus*) is another species that does well on chalk soils. But the best lawns are composed of a selection of grasses with different habits that together make good turf. It is difficult to obtain single varieties of grass seed, and it is unwise to sow a single variety, or to create your own mixtures. It is preferable to buy a mixture from a good seedsman (you can look for mixtures containing ryegrass or crested dog's tail), and to depend on cultivation to overcome any problems associated with the alkalinity of your soil.

Foliar feeding is best done on dull days or in the evening, to reduce the likelihood of scorching the leaves. Calm weather helps too, as the solution is likely to remain on the foliage for longer.

If manganese deficiency is suspected, try a foliar spray of manganese sulphate at a rate of 15g to 10 litres (½ oz to 2 gallons) of water. Repeat again a few weeks later if it seems to be effective.

If you are incurably experimental, or simply don't want to give up the chance to grow a lime-hater to which you are particularly attached, it will also be necessary to use chelated iron each season.

Chelated or sequestered iron (Sequestrene is one trade name to look for) won't be locked up by the high pH. It will remain available to the plants for many months, perhaps the whole season. Sequestered manganese and magnesium are also available, and you can buy 'tonics' that contain all these sequestered elements plus a number of trace elements such as molybdenum.

These preparations are usually added to water and then applied to the soil around the affected plants, but follow the manufacturer's instructions. Trees and large bushes will probably need treating twice in a season, smaller plants perhaps just the once. If you have just a few plants to treat this way, you may consider it well worth the cost, but it can become expensive if you attempt to treat large areas with chelates.

There's another form of trace elements that can be useful on alkaline soils, the so-called fritted trace elements. These contain manganese, iron, zinc, copper, boron, and molybdenum bonded to glass beads. The nutrients are released only slowly, and continue to feed the plants for a long period (at least for a growing season). The granules must be spread evenly around the area of root growth, and for established trees it may be necessary to bore small holes around the edge of the root area in which to insert the chemicals.

Although you will find chelated (sequestered) products in most garden centres, it is usually more difficult to find fritted trace elements. They are, however, much less important than the chelates in controlling lime-induced deficiencies.

MULCHING

Mulching is something always advocated but all too

Fig 17. It makes sense to give newly planted trees the best start in life. A tree guard will help to protect it from animals, and a mulch will help to conserve moisture – especially important on thin chalk soils.

seldom practised. It's a good idea on almost any soil, but especially so on shallow chalk soils, where it can gradually increase depth and build up a layer of less alkaline soil.

Mulching is an odd term. It comes from a German dialect word *Molsch,* meaning soft and beginning to decay. That aptly describes mulches of animal manures, garden compost, spent hops, and the like. But the term has also come to include anything that provides a barrier to weeds and cuts down moisture loss through evaporation, even if the material rots only slowly or not at all: peat, pulverized bark, and even plastic and other synthetic sheets.

The first group, those that rot down to provide humus for the soil, are the best, because they provide nutrients and slowly improve the structure of the soil, as well as acting as a physical barrier in the short-term. Peats are useful as a mulch on alkaline soils, because they can help to make the soil more acid as they become incorporated into the soil. The purely barrier types, such as black polythene, won't do much for soil fertility, but they still play an important role in suppressing weed competition (especially important while plants are becoming established) and help to retain soil moisture.

Bulky mulches that gradually rot down should be replaced or topped up annually. To be effective at suppressing weeds, they need to be at least 5 cm (2 in) thick. Peat and pulverized bark will need topping up from time to time to maintain a similar thickness. There is the bonus of an attractive appearance with both of these materials, which look much better than bare soil.

Never apply a mulch to dry soil – unless the rain is very heavy it will simply be absorbed by the mulch and little will penetrate to the soil beneath. Although moisture will eventually reach the soil after a period of prolonged rain, in the meantime the plants in an already dry soil will suffer. So if the ground is not already wet, soak it with the hose before mulching.

Mulches can encourage slugs and snails. Trees and shrubs usually survive unscathed, but if you are mulching around vulnerable herbaceous plants you may feel that it is worth sprinkling a little slug bait around them first, even though this will not have a long-lasting effect. Slug pellets which are based on methiocarb are very effective.

WATERING

Whether you garden on a limy clay, a limy sand, or a shallow chalk soil, summer drought is likely to be a problem for many plants. Watering is fun for a few minutes but can soon become a tedious chore, so it's worth finding long-term solutions.

Mulching will help to conserve moisture and reduce the demands for more water, but there's a limit to how much you can mulch. In the vegetable garden you may have to depend more on cutting down water loss through weed competition, for instance. Constant hoeing may help.

Growing drought-resistant plants, many of which are recommended in this book, will also cut down the need to water. But there will still be many plants that will become stressed and perform poorly if not watered during a dry spell.

Water needs to be applied in plenty, albeit not very frequently, rather than lots of insubstantial sprinklings. If you apply only enough water to dampen the top centimetre or two, most of it will probably be lost through evaporation before it reaches the root zones for the plants to benefit. Using a watering-can is so tiring that the chances are you won't apply sufficient water to do much good. Watering-cans are fine for watering planting holes, and perhaps for applying liquid feeds, but they are not the answer for serious watering.

The first essential is an outdoor tap, and a good length of hose (preferably one that you can unwind and rewind easily). You'll feel more inclined to water when necessary if the job's made as easy as possible.

A pop-up sprinkler system in the flower beds and lawn is ideal, but relatively few of us are willing to go to the expense and trouble of installing this kind of system. But you could improvise by having more or less permanently laid hoses, which you will have to lay in small trenches beneath the beds and perhaps under paths. For little extra cost they could have fixed-jet spray heads permanently fitted, and all you would need to do would be to connect a short length of hose from the tap to the delivery hose. With modern click-fit connectors this is a quick and simple job. The hoses may have to be replaced after a few years, but this simple DIY system is a compromise between a proper fixed system and having to trail a hose around the garden each time you want to water.

Unless the garden is very small, you probably won't be able to water all of it. It's very worthwhile having a sprinkler on the vegetable plot too: many crops, such as peas, are not worthwhile unless you can ensure adequate soil moisture at critical times. Concentrate also on beds of annuals, and newly planted trees and shrubs. If a lush green lawn is important to you, it will be essential to water the lawn during dry spells – especially if you are using fertilizers or lawn weedkillers. The grass will, however, recover in any case after heavy rain; plants that are not yet properly established may perish.

PPENDIX

WHERE TO SEE CHALK GARDENS

If you are looking for inspiration from other gardens, perhaps for good planting combinations or simply to see first hand the range of plants that will do well on chalk and limestone, there are plenty of good gardens to visit.

In Britain we are fortunate in having many excellent gardens open to the public, including many under the National Gardens Scheme. Gardens open under this scheme have not been included here because they are generally open to the public for a limited period during the year, and the days may vary from year to year. It's worth consulting the current yearbook, looking under known chalk or limestone areas for gardens described as being on these soils. You will, for instance find many in that category on the South Downs listed under Sussex, and more under Wiltshire. If you have a chalk or limestone garden, you will know the area under which to check.

Garden visiting is a wonderful pastime anyway, so it makes sense to try to fit in a few visits to chalk gardens on your holidays and when tra-velling around the country. Some of the famous ones will be found in the list below, and all are well worth visiting for their general horticultural merit anyway. The list is by no means exhaustive.

A word of warning. Don't assume that all parts of these chalk or limestone gardens are alkaline. Some areas may have been dressed with top-soil imported from elsewhere, and in others there may be neutral or even acid areas of the garden that have been achieved after years of culti-vation. If a plant is doing well in any of these gardens, it does not necessarily follow that it will do well in yours.

The gardens listed here are open for at least several months of the year, but not necessarily every day. Where a telephone number is given, check opening times and exact location.

Don't forget to take a note-book and pencil with you when you go garden visiting in order to jot down names of plants that appeal to you. Also make notes of any par-ticularly attractive plant associations that you come across.

Anglesey Abbey, Lode, Cambridgeshire
6 miles NE of Cambridge. Trees, shrubs, herbaceous perennials. A National Trust garden.
Tel: Cambridge (0223) 811200.

Barnsley House Garden, nr Cirencester, Gloucestershire
4 miles NE of Cirencester, on A433. Trees, shrubs, roses, herbaceous plants, laburnum walk, herbs, decorative vegetable garden.
Tel: Bibury (028574) 281

Bristol Zoological Garden, Bristol, Avon
Clifton, Bristol. Specimen trees, herbaceous plants, rock garden, summer bedding.
Tel: Bristol (0272) 738951

Cambridge University Botanic Garden, Cambridge
Near junction of A10 and A604. An interesting botanic garden on an alluvial river bed overlying a chalk subsoil, with an outstanding carboniferous limestone rock garden.
Tel: Cambridge (0223) 336265

Claverton Manor, nr Bath, Avon
Signposted from Bath. The American Museum in Britain. Roses, herbaceous plants, herb garden.
Tel: Bath (0225) 60503

Hidcote Manor Gardens, Hidcote Bartrim, Gloucestershire
4 miles NE of Chipping Campden. Trees, shrubs, herbaceous borders, old-fashioned roses. A National Trust garden.
Tel: Mickleton (0386) 438333

Highdown Gardens, Goring-by-Sea, West Sussex
3 miles W of Worthing. Trees, shrubs, bulbs, peonies, herbaceous plants.
Tel: Worthing (0903) 501054

Kiftsgate Court Garden, Chipping Campden, Gloucestershire
East of Mickleton. Shrubs, old roses.
Tel: Mickleton (0386) 438777

Levens Hall, Kendal, Cumbria
5 miles S of Kendal. Shrubs, topiary.
Tel: Sedgwick (0448) 60321

**Mottisfont Abbey,
nr Romsey, Hampshire**
4-5 miles NW of Romsey. Trees, herbaceous borders, old-fashioned roses. A National Trust garden.
Tel: Lockerley (0794) 40757

**Northbourne Court,
nr Deal, Kent**
3 miles west of Deal. Grey foliage and mixed borders, walled garden and terraces.
Tel: Deal (0304) 360813

**Polesden Lacey,
nr Dorking, Surrey**
3 miles NW of Dorking. Shrubs, roses, herbaceous borders. A National Trust garden.
Tel: Bookham (0372) 52048

**Preston Manor Park,
Brighton, East Sussex**
On A23 north of Brighton. Large park with rose garden, enclosed garden, garden for the blind, and adjoining rock garden.

**Pusey House Gardens,
nr Faringdon, Oxfordshire**
5 miles E of Faringdon. Herbaceous borders, walled gardens, shrubs, trees, roses.
Tel: Buckland (036787) 222.

**Sizergh Castle Garden,
Sedgwick, Cumbria**
4 miles S of Kendal. Large limestone rock garden. Hardy fern collection and mature dwarf conifers. Herbaceous and groundcover plants. A National Trust garden.
Tel: Sedgwick (05395) 60070

**Snowshill Manor,
nr Broadway,
Worcestershire**
3 miles S of Broadway. Herbaceous borders. A National Trust Garden.
Tel: Broadway (0386) 852410

**Uppark, South Harting,
Hampshire**
5 miles SE of Petersfield. Shrubs, roses, mixed borders, climbing plants. A National Trust garden.
Tel: Harting (073085) 317

BIBLIOGRAPHY

BERRISFORD, JUDITH M. *Gardening on Lime* Faber, 1963
BERTRAM ANDERSON, E. *Gardening on Chalk and Limestone* Collingridge, 1965
FISH, MARJORY *Gardening on Clay and Lime* David and Charles, 1970
Hillier's Manual of Trees and Shrubs David and Charles, 1981
LLOYD, CHRISTOPHER *Gardening on Chalk and Lime* Pan, 1969
Notcutt's Nursery Book of Plants
STERN, F.C. *A Chalk Garden* Nelson, 1960

ACKNOWLEDGMENTS

The publishers are grateful to the following for kindly granting permission for their photographs to be included in this book: Pat Brindley (pp 23, 75, 94, 115); John Glover (pp 78, 103, 107); Peter McHoy (pp 2/3, 7, 31); Photos Horticultural (pp 38, 54, 59, 66, 71, 83, 86, 87, 102, 111) and Harry Smith (pp 11, 14, 15, 18, 30, 39, 43, 46, 62, 70, 106).

All line drawings by Ann Winterbotham.